A GUY'S JOURNEY TO
MANHOOD

Doug Marsh

GPH®

Gospel Publishing House
Springfield, Missouri
02-0618

We would like to express our deep appreciation to Rev. Lloyd Marsh for allowing Royal Rangers to adapt "Making New Disciples" without restrictions on pages 163–170. Copyrighted material 2008 Rev. Lloyd D. Marsh. All rights reserved. Used by permission. www.makenewdisciples.com

We would like to express our deep appreciation to Matt McPherson for allowing Royal Rangers to use unaltered "The Salvation Poem" on pages 60–62. Copyrighted material 2008 IMF Productions. All rights reserved. Used by permission. www.thesalvationpoem.com

International Standard Book Number: 978-1-60731-314-4

Printed in United States of America

Contents

Introduction

My Story

We are all born into God's story.
Let me tell you my part.

Peru

I was born on the beach in Lima, Peru in South America. Well, the hospital was actually on the beach anyway. My mom and dad were serving as Assemblies of God missionaries when I came along to join my five-year-old sister and seven-year-old brother.

Doug Marsh

God had called my parents to start churches around Puno, Peru where they had none. It's on the shore of a big lake high in the Andes Mountains, called Lago Titicaca.

After starting their first churches, they established a Bible school in the city of Puno to train men and woman to be pastors. The amazing Quichua people they ministered to were farmers. The

My family on the "floating islands" near Puno, Peru.

school met for only four months each year; classes started right after the planting season and continued until just before harvest.

When classes weren't in session, we would travel three-to-six months in the back of our camper. There were six of us—my family and our volunteer teacher from Texas who lived with us and homeschooled us. Every night we would have a candlelit dinner because electricity was scarce.

After dinner the six of us would help clean up our beloved home on wheels, and all but my parents would wait outside so they could prepare for bed. When they were ready, they would thump twice on the inside wall of the camper with their hand to signal that my sister and our teacher could climb in and get ready. They would convert the table where we had just eaten into a bed and sleep there. My brother got the bunk over them. And, me, the youngest of the family, well, you know where I slept, right? You got it. On the floor!

My bed was special. My dad received generous funds to print gospel literature that helped us tell Jesus' story in the local language. I slept on top of those boxes every night. At the start of our journey the boxes were full and my bed was firm. But as the literature was distributed, my bed got lumpy. But I wouldn't have traded it for anything; I liked the adventure of traveling in the

Andes, and we loved the people dearly. I spent my nights on the Word of God, literally.

When we were not on the road, my dad and I had a morning tradition. We called it our Think Pill Session. (Sounds so official, doesn't it?) I'd take a glass of Coke for each of us to my dad's office. Hidden behind his books on a shelf out of my reach, dad kept a big stash of Peruvian candies similar to M&Ms. For about ten minutes we'd down some chocolate and drink Coke. It was the highlight of my day as a kid.

One morning I went into his office for our Think Pill Session. Rather than let me take the seat I normally did, my dad called me over to sit on his lap. He pointed and instructed me to open his lower desk drawer. Inside there was a small package with my name on it from America. I was so excited! It was my first piece of mail.

Inside was a thin booklet that I immediately discarded in favor of the colorfully embroidered patch inside. I'd never seen it before but immediately liked it. I jumped off my dad's lap and took off with my new toy, but he caught me and explained I'd have to earn the patch. Earn it? What's that about? He explained what each of the colorful points meant, and once I could recite them from memory, I'd officially be a Royal Ranger—a program that would teach me how to become a godly man.

I was motivated. I wanted to become a real man! The Andean farmers our family served impressed me. They were tough. They planted high in the mountains and raised animals in very harsh conditions. I admired my dad, too. He was a preacher and a teacher in a place where God's Word had never been heard. His love and passion inspired me. I wanted to be a real man.

Two weeks later I had met the requirements, and my dad pinned that patch on my shirt. In that moment, God did something supernatural in my heart—He placed a seed of understanding of the man I'd grow into, and I knew that I knew God wanted me to become a missionary and a minister who helped boys become godly men.

As you know, it takes time for a seed to germinate, grow, and produce fruit. I had a lot of learning to do still. I was only six years old. Never doubt that God speaks to you in your youth.

Bolivia

By the time I was seven years old, my parents had already served in Peru for sixteen years. The work was strong. Sixteen churches and the Bible school had been established. The leaders were healthy and taking the work to places we could not reach. The national political conditions were changing. It was time to move. God was leading my parents to a new place of service. We moved from Peru to Bolivia, which is on the other side of Lago Titicaca. For the next eleven years, I'd call its capital city, La Paz, my home.

Admittedly, I was a little confused by the move at first. What would happen to our father-son times of learning about becoming a godly man? Can you do that in a new place? Funny the questions you ask as a kid, isn't it? Of course, I'd eventually learn that God can shape you into the man He wants regardless of the place or circumstances of your life—and that is something worth remembering. Little did I know that God had big plans for me, stirred in with some smiles, some tears, and lots of learning.

Teacher Comments
Fourth Quarter

Doug has continued to try hard during the past quarter but his skills and grasp of concepts are significantly below grade level. It is my recommendation that Doug remain in the Fourth Grade during 1981–82.

Teacher comment from my 4th grade report card.
These are the words that changed my life.

The biggest change that I faced was school. For the first time ever, I was not the only student in the classroom. I had been homeschooled and would now be in a classroom with twenty to thirty others! Who are these beautiful creatures? They call them girls? Wow, amazing. I've got to meet them, all of them! Recess? What is that? Time for king of the mountain! Soccer and more soccer. Physical education? Is that really a class? Love it, can't get enough of that! After school activities? More soccer, you say? I am there!

See what's missing? By the time I finished fourth grade, I was excelling at everything in school except academics. Then came the biggest blow of my childhood. I was required to repeat the fourth grade. It's not like I didn't see it coming. The poor grades, the tutoring that interrupted my love of sports and time with friends, the warnings from my parents and teachers should have gotten my attention, but they didn't.

I've never cried so long or loud in my life. What would my friends think? I was embarrassed. I was disappointed in myself. But over the summer months and with the help of my parents and a few friends, I chose to "man-up" to my failure. I stopped blaming others and took responsibility. I stopped telling myself I was a failure—a script my dad would not allow me to play over and over in my head. After all, the line you believe determines your future. If that line is a lie, you're doomed. If it's truth, your future is sure.

My mom and dad helped me realize how capable I was but that my priorities had been out of line. I'd also let myself drift spiritually, going through the motions. Life had become all fun and games, all adventure and no work or discipline. A balance was needed. But to bring that balance, I'd have to sacrifice lots of fun to catch up.

That first day back at school was tough. Last year's third-graders, who had looked up to me (or feared me) on the playground, were now my fourth-grade classmates. They didn't mind rubbing my nose in my failure. Last year's peers, now fifth-graders, joined the chorus. It was not easy! But my parents had a plan, I knew what it was, and we were going to show everyone what I was made of.

I repeated and successfully completed the fourth grade and with the additional help of a tutor achieved the standardized scores in all subjects expected of a boy ready to enter the fifth grade. I'll never forget the name of my fourth-grade teacher, Señora Vientemillas. She had married a man from Spain whose last name literally meant twenty miles!

Next, things got really good. I dropped out of school. Well, kind of. I returned to homeschooling again. I'd complete fifth and sixth grades in one year. No small task!

After my second fourth-grade adventure, I sacrificed my summer and started fifth grade two weeks later and finished just before Christmas. After another short break, I started sixth grade and entered the seventh grade to rejoin my original class. You should have been there the day I walked back on campus. The look on my classmates' faces was priceless.

Through it I learned that God could help you overcome life's biggest setbacks. These challenges serve the purpose of making us strong.

My senior year of high school.

Through all this, I was on a quest to become God's man. I was active in Royal Rangers and had some outstanding mentors who modeled Christlike behavior and spoke words of encouragement and life into me. One such leader was David North, a college student called to minister to young men. I had shared with some people my dreams for the future and had grown discouraged by their responses. I risked sharing with one more person, David, and he has been a source of encouragement in my life now for over twenty-five years.

The church I was attending closed Royal Rangers down because of some difficulties. I was discouraged and thought my days in the program were over. The encouragement from David and my parents challenged me to find a way to make something good come out of the situation. It was a call from a pastor who asked if I could help their church start Royal Rangers that set things in motion.

I was fourteen-years-old and asked to train grown men in La Paz, Bolivia, how to mentor boys. I was terrified, but refused to admit it. I accepted the pastor's invitation and started training and strategizing with his leaders how we would reach the boys and young men in their community and shape them into godly men. About three months later, we launched an outreach and held our first meeting with eighty in attendance. I thought for sure we would whittle that down to about thirty or even twenty. But, no, it only grew. Then other pastors called, and the story repeated itself over and over again. By the time high school graduation rolled around, I had started thirty-three groups and trained over 125 leaders who were influencing over a thousand boys for Christ each and every week all across Bolivia.

Naturally, during those high school years, I was doing what every teen guy does: I was dreaming about the future and trying my best to land on some concrete plans. I knew what my heart was calling me to but didn't know how to get there or even know *if* I could get there. I wanted to be a missionary who could inspire and train leaders everywhere to mentor future men of God.

College

God unexpectedly made things fall in place. It's something Jesus promises to do when you "seek first his kingdom and his righteousness, and all these things will be given to you as well" (Matthew 6:33). King David wrote, "The Lord makes firm the steps of the one who delights in him" (Psalm 37:23). I was washing my dad's car one afternoon when he ran out to the drive, excitedly shouting, "Doug, Doug, you've got a phone call from Springfield, Missouri." Living in Bolivia, we didn't get too many calls from America because it was extremely expensive. So I hustled in while drying my hands so I wouldn't get the phone wet. All the while I'm thinking to myself, "What have I done wrong to get a call from the Assemblies of God headquarters? I'm just a teen; these calls are for my dad!"

On the line was George Davis, one of my most-beloved mentors. He said, "Doug, let's keep this short. I've got three questions for you:

"First, do you plan to attend Central Bible College when you graduate from high school?" The answer was yes. In fact, just days earlier I had been accepted.

"Second, will you need a job?" I thought to myself, *Duh!* but answered respectfully, "Yes, sir."

"Third, would you consider being the training coordinator for Royal Rangers in Latin America and the Caribbean and helping me develop the curricular and training resources for the whole region?" I immediately shouted, "Yes!"

The Lord opened doors that quickly. During the four years I attended college, I was able to travel all over Mexico, Central and South America, and the Caribbean training leaders to shape the next generation of men. During these college days, I also met and married the fairest lady of the entire universe. We moved to Costa Rica in Central America as Assemblies of God missionaries shortly after graduating from college.

World

During the nine years we lived and served in Costa Rica, the Lord enabled us to build ministries to men and boys in nineteen Latin American countries. We also established Camp Summit, an eighty-acre training and discipleship center, designed to challenge and inspire men and boys to love God with their whole hearts and serve others selflessly. Our two children, Jon and Katelyn, were also born while we lived there.

Then in 2002, our leadership asked us to expand our ministry globally by starting Royal Rangers International (RRI). So we entered a new season of adventure and challenge. Today, we are ministering in over eighty-six nations and every sign points to continued growth. It's so amazing to be part of what God is doing in the lives of young people on every continent.

The Lord then threw us our greatest surprise in 2007. The executive leadership of the Assemblies of God asked if I would also lead the Royal Rangers ministry in the United States. What a ride it's been! Our role is unique as we continue as missionaries while also serving as members of the National Leadership and Resource Center, representing their commitment to the value of mentoring future men. To see this value also taking root in so many churches across the nation is humbling.

You

The point of my story is this: "The one who calls you is faithful, and he will do it" (1 Thessalonians 5:24). God has dreams for your life that would absolutely blow your mind if He sat next to you and shared them all in one setting! So walk with God, and He will help you reach your dreams! God loves to fulfill the desires of boys and young men who fear Him. (See Psalm 145:19.)

Another thing I hope you have concluded from reading my story is that this book represents a quest of my own. My whole life I've asked God to shape me into His man, and this is the journey I'm on. I've also asked Him to help me influence millions of boys and young men to avoid the pitfalls of immature manhood. So as you read the pages ahead, in a real sense, we are on a journey together to manhood.

Are you ready?

Choose Your Path

"Be very careful . . . to love the Lord your God, to walk in obedience to him, to keep his commands, to hold fast to him and to serve him with all your heart and with all your soul."

—Joshua 22:5

CHAPTER 1

On Becoming a Man

Every boy dreams of becoming a man—I know I did. But when do you become a man? Does that happen when you grow facial hair? When you learn to drive? When you turn twenty-one? What is the secret to becoming a man?

Becoming God's Man

The measure of a man is found in his maturity. Maturity is the ability to accept responsibility—to be dependable, to do what you say you'll do, and to do what you are expected to do. Showing maturity has little to do with physical size, strength, age, or social status.

As a young child, you first learned to accept responsibility for yourself. You learned to dress yourself and brush your own teeth. About that same time, you learned to assume responsibility for your surroundings by picking up after yourself and making your bed. Then you started learning to assume responsibility for others around you by being polite, offering a willing hand to help others, and being kind and thoughtful. So you matured by accepting responsibility for yourself, and later, by being focused on the needs of others. Your maturity increases as you accept more responsibility.

It is cute to watch a one-year-old toss and leave his toys on the floor; when a fifteen-year-old does that, we call it immaturity. However, if that same young man is responsible, he gains the admiration of peers and adults alike.

> The journey to mature manhood is accepting responsibility for yourself and for others by serving them.

The apostle Paul told Titus, a young church leader, to "encourage the young men to be self-controlled" (Titus 2:6). In other words, men need to be mature. The journey to maturity is accepting responsibility for yourself and for others by serving them.

Who to Model

Jesus is the perfect example of what it means to be a man. He was 100 percent God and 100 percent man. He was tempted like you are in every way, yet He never gave into it! He faced every temptation you have faced, and stood strong. (See Hebrews 4:15.) Jesus accepted responsibility for himself—for His actions, for the development of His character, and for the fulfillment of His life purpose.

Later, He died on a cross to pay the price for the sins of the entire world. Since He never sinned, He didn't need to die for himself. Jesus took responsibility for others and their sins. If He hadn't, people would have to die for their own sins. In doing this, He served them.

Jesus is the perfect picture of a man—a strong man! He took responsibility for himself in every way: His words, His actions, His attitudes, His mental growth, His physical development, His spiritual influence, and His character. Then, He assumed responsibility for others by giving His life for their sins.

You Can Be a Real Man

Jesus is our model of maturity and responsibility. He calls us to be just like Him. Jesus expects us to accept responsibility for ourselves. It starts by admitting our human condition—separated from God by our sin. Many men think taking responsibility for themselves equals living life their own way. Real men know that taking responsibility begins with recognizing they are sinners in need of a Savior.

Once men realize their need for a Savior, they submit to His leadership. Jesus trains them to live real and full lives; they allow Him to shape their character to match His. Being like Jesus is what it means to be a real man. Following Him as your daily leader and loving Him with your whole heart is what it takes to become like Him.

Jesus grew from a boy into a young man, just like you. He became a strong and confident man. He changed the course of history by dying on a cross and rising from the dead to save those who chose to follow Him. What was His secret? The Gospel of John tells us: Jesus didn't live His life His own way; instead He lived it the way His Heavenly Father wanted Him to live it. (See John 6:38.)

You have been created for a special purpose, and who knows your design better than God? That's why it is so important to accept responsibility by recognizing that you become a real man as you follow His leadership in your life. When you love Him more than you love yourself, you become even more like Him.

As you follow Jesus, He will shape your character. He will help you grow into a strong and confident man. He will show you God's great purpose for you, and give your life a worthy cause. Jesus' cause was to save you from your sin so you could become the best possible version of you. But He could not have accepted responsibility for you if He had not

> "The more alive you allow Christ to become in you, the more real you'll become." —Romans 6:11 (author paraphrase).

accepted responsibility for himself first—the responsibility to live life God's way instead of His own way.

The Choice Is Your Responsibility

You are at the starting line of your journey to manhood. Like every journey, it begins by choosing your path. Unfortunately, many boys choose to go their own way. The Bible tells us we are like sheep that have gone astray; we have lived life our own way (Isaiah 53:6). But the result of living life our own way is sad and predictable. It leads to loss, death, and separation from God (Romans 3:23).

The better path is to follow Christ. It is the only true path to becoming a real man. Choosing this path leads to a full life that money and fame can never buy. It leads to the greatest gift; one you get only by following Jesus—the gift of eternal life (Romans 6:23).

So every day you have a choice to make. Who will you follow? Following your own way leads to death. Choosing Jesus leads to life. This is a choice you must make yourself. It is your responsibility. Your choice has consequences. Following your own path will lead to immature manhood, loss, and death. Following Jesus will lead to mature manhood, fulfillment, and life. Choose life!

Journey in the Company of Men

If you have chosen to follow Christ, congratulations are in order. Now for some really important advice—don't take this journey alone! Yes, Christ is always with you, but He intends for you to undertake this quest in the company of men.

True manhood is bestowed upon you in the company of godly men. Being inspired by a book you read, a story you hear, or a movie you watch won't make you a man by itself. Following God's path, with other godly men by your side, will make you a real man.

This book is a road map for every guy's journey to manhood. Use it alone and you'll be inspired for a season. But follow it with other committed young men of God under the mentorship of godly men, and it will positively influence the course of your whole life.

Like any map, you're going to need it for the whole journey. Becoming the man God intends is not something accomplished in a day; it is a lifelong pursuit. The foundations you establish in your youth are arguably the most important. Go through this material carefully and refer to it often. Review it to keep it fresh in your mind. Study it the way you might a map when you've ventured deep in the wilderness and want to know the location of every water source, river crossing, mountain, valley, and cliff.

You are on a lifelong journey. Establish strong foundations and do it early in life. Travel with godly men and guys your age, because manhood is granted to you as you journey with a band of brothers who are in pursuit of Christlike manhood.

In Your Own Words:

In the course of our journey together, I'll ask you some important questions. Don't skip over them. It's important you give them full consideration and give them expression in your own words.

1. Have you chosen to follow Christ? If so, can you describe the time, place, and reasons you did?

2. Who will take this journey with you? Your dad? Mentors at church? What about your peers?

In My Experience:

Throughout this book, you will find sections entitled, "In My Experience." In them I share the good, the bad, and at times the ugly truths about my life. I hope the experiences I share will help you interact with the material.

I've done it right, and I've blown it. There are times I've ventured out on this manhood journey in the company of men and other times I've gone it alone. There is an old African proverb that says, "If you want to go fast, go alone. But if you want to go far, go in the company of others." As I look back on my life, I must admit the proverb is true.

My dad was my greatest mentor. As soon as the Friday afternoon dismissal bell rang, he was waiting outside my high school. We lived overseas and would go blow some money on imported American junk food—sometimes we could even find Dr. Pepper, which wasn't an easy task in Bolivia. As we savored the sugar and carbs, we talked about everything—girls (of course!), cars, money, church, witnessing, college, dreams, and so much more. My dad, and other adult mentors, helped me go further and soar higher. I feel their influence to this day.

My freshman year was one of those seasons when I journeyed without godly peers at my side. It was tough! It wasn't that I intended to, but few of them were serving the Lord. I was lonely and often felt lost. I took comfort in the chorus an old, old song written way back in 1873 by Philip P. Bliss for his boys' Sunday School class. In it, he urged them to "Dare to Be a Daniel" and to stand firm for God when circumstances demand it.

I dreaded the thought but braced myself to walk the halls of my high school alone. Then I discovered the words to the entire song. The lyrics helped me realize there would always be times I'd need to stand alone and firm. But even Daniel had a band of brothers. So I prayed for a friend, and God answered. For the next two years, David Thomas and I challenged and inspired each other. It was as the Old Testament wisdom writer described: "iron sharpening iron" (Proverbs 27:17).

That's how it should be. I've learned from the good and the bad to journey with others so we can challenge one another. Godly men make each other better. It's how men become men.

Dare to Be a Daniel

Standing by a purpose true,
Heeding God's command,
Honor them, the faithful few!
All hail to Daniel's band!

Chorus:
Dare to be a Daniel,
Dare to stand alone!
Dare to have a purpose firm!
Dare to make it known.

Many mighty men are lost
Daring not to stand,
Who for God had been a host
By joining Daniel's band.

Many giants, great and tall,
Stalking through the land,
Headlong to the earth would fall,
If met by Daniel's band.

Hold the Gospel banner high!
On to vict'ry grand!
Satan and his hosts defy,
And shout for Daniel's band.

—Philip Bliss, 1873

CHAPTER 2

How God Builds a Real Man

Being a Christian young man is about becoming the best version of you possible. You were born a male, and God wants you to become an extraordinary man!

In building men, God has never deviated from His pattern. He has always built men by starting them out as boys. Even when He sent His own Son, Jesus, He didn't change His plan. He started Jesus as a Baby born in a barn, raised in a small town with His dad who was a carpenter, and developed like every other boy and young man.

So God always builds men from the same starting point. Guys love it when we start showing signs that we are becoming men—deeper voice, stronger muscles, and facial hair.

Obviously, most of these signs are physical, and will naturally happen with a healthy diet, exercise, and sleep. However, the inside stuff that makes you a godly man is not so automatic. It only develops in you if you put effort into it. You must be careful not to allow the outward growth of your body to overshadow the inward development of your character.

Your parents, your pastors, your mentors, and other godly influences can encourage you to develop the inside stuff, but they can't do it for you. It is your responsibility. You must choose to mature into an outstanding man of God.

God designed young men everywhere to want three things, summarized in the word *ACT*— ADVENTUROUS fun, strength of CHARACTER, and a deeply personal TASK, or purpose, to live for. He uses these to build boys and young men so they get their ACT together and become exceptional men if they will let Him.

God Builds Men on Adventure

When God builds men, He starts with ADVENTURE. Do you like to hike, hunt, or fish? Play ball or watch sports? Listen to or play your music? Take photos, edit videos, or produce podcasts? Build or fix things? These are fun things us guys like to do. We dream of adventure—going places, testing our limits, doing things that matter, and having fun! Do you realize God made you to enjoy adventure? He did! The Bible says God rides on the clouds and wind, speaks in the thunder, and plays in the rain (Deuteronomy 33:26; Psalms 68:33; 104:3; 135:7). God has fun, and so can you.

The greatest adventure God gives you is your life, but we should never attempt to do life on our own. God asks you to go on adventures with Him. This requires faith. Faith is trust—trust that God will never let you down, leave you behind, or forget about you. That sounds risky, doesn't it? But that is the very nature of adventure. It is characterized by a measure of fear of the unseen or the unknown. That is exactly what makes it so fun, and without it, your Christian life will be boring. The cure is adventure!

When you choose to follow Christ, it will always be an adventure. He will ask you to do things that will require you to trust Him. Following Him will far surpass any adrenaline rush you could create for yourself. Only when you experience His adventures will you truly know God. Until you head out with Him, God will be a distant, impersonal, and faceless figure. However, when you choose to trust Him, you will really know Him.

Adventuring with God means loving Him and loving others as much as you love yourself. Jesus called this the Great Commandment. Take note of this! Adventuring with God is not optional. It is a command. It's the way God builds a man. No adventure? No journey to manhood!

The Great Commandment
"Love the Lord your God with all your heart and with all your soul and with all your mind and with all your strength."
—Mark 12:30

Real men risk it all to follow God. They learn to love Him with everything they have and to love others as much as they love themselves. Young men who play it safe grow physically as men but remain immature boys on the inside. God transforms boys into men on adventures. It's pure adrenaline, on-your-feet-learning with God. It's never boring and always exciting; even the routine disciplines can be filled with excitement. Trust God and follow Him. You won't be disappointed.

What kind of adventures do you expect God to bring your way? You might start a business, play a sport, or become a missionary, pastor, or evangelist. Whatever it is, you can be sure it will be exciting, risky, and challenging, and it will shape you into a godly man.

God Forges Men's Character in Battle

While on your adventure, God adds CHARACTER as He builds you into a man. Character is our inside strength that comes in the form of brainpower, creative talents and abilities, emotional stability, and moral and spiritual strength to make the right choices. This strength of character is designed to help you serve others, defend the defenseless, and to protect the ones we love.

Growing strong on the inside is not something you can do on our own. You have to rely on the Holy Spirit to shape you from the inside out. The real you is the inside you. When you ask Jesus to come into your heart, to forgive your sins, and to be your Friend and the Leader of your life, His Spirit lives inside you. Then, if you let Him, the Holy Spirit will work on you and shape you to be more and more like Jesus. How awesome is that? You can be made strong and powerful like Jesus!

Have you ever realized it is easier to pull people down than it is to lift them up? It takes real strength and courage to lift people, and only the weight of unkind actions, words, and attitudes to hold them down. Guys who hold others back are weak inside. However, guys who have character and who lift others are truly strong. It takes character to be a real man who cares about and builds up his inner strength.

The Great Empowerment

"You will receive power when the Holy Spirit comes on you; and you will be my witnesses in Jerusalem, and in all Judea and Samaria, and to the ends of the earth."
—Acts 1:8

The Holy Spirit will make you strong on the inside. This is the Great Empowerment—the Holy Spirit gives you power for life and ministry, builds your character, and focuses your God-given abilities. He gives you the inside stuff that makes you truly strong. The Holy Spirit has unlimited strength, and He wants to share it all with you if you will let Him.

God Reveals Men's Life Task

God plants into men a drive to accomplish a special TASK. This gives you direction and purpose. Adventure and strength focused on a special task makes you a real man.

Some guys love adventure only for the opportunity to have fun. These are the guys who take advantage of others and ultimately wreck their own futures. Think about Samson, the Old Testament judge, who landed himself in a work prison, lost his

God-given strength, and had his eyes gouged out. God had given him a love for ADVENTURE and challenge plus great physical and moral CHARACTER for the TASK of delivering his nation from the grip of their oppressors. But he played games with God, preferring to create his own adventure rather than trusting God to lead him on a truly great adventure. He used his strength for selfish gain rather than to accomplish his special task of serving others.

Who are good examples in your life of a godly adventure toward manhood? Look for someone who loves adventure, is morally and spiritually strong, and is focused on serving family, the church, and you! Godly men focus their ADVENTURE and CHARACTER strength on a special TASK, or purpose—being God's allies to tell the whole world about His love. We call this the Great Commission, the awesome task of showing everyone in the whole world God's amazing love. God will show you your special role in this task as you obediently go on adventure with Him.

The Great Commission
"Therefore go and make disciples of all nations, baptizing them in the name of the Father and of the Son and of the Holy Spirit, and teaching them to obey everything I have commanded you. And surely I am with you always, to the very end of the age."
—Matthew 28:19–20

Now that you know how God builds a real man, are you willing to go on adventure with Him? Are you willing to let the Holy Spirit shape your character? Are you willing to assume your special task in life? Get your ACT together, become a man! Let God build your life. If you do, it will be full of ADVENTURE, strong CHARACTER, and a special TASK. That is what is required to become the best version of you, the best man you can be. You were born a male, but that alone won't make you a real man. Let God shape you into the extraordinary man He wants you to become.

In Your Own Words:

1. Is your Christian walk an adventure? Why or why not?

2. Can you name public figures you admire because of their character? How about church leaders, parents, teachers, or coaches?

3. God has a task for you. What are your dreams?

In My Experience:

I've encouraged the spiritual development of boys and young men for years. In my experience, some boys think it is harder than it really is. Others think it is easier.

Here's what I've learned. Jesus wants a relationship with you. He will not weigh you down with burdens. He offers real and full life. That's the adventure! But the truth is that life is hard. God does not remove us from hardship, but He walks through it with us and makes us stronger because of it. A wise person once said, "God will not protect you from what He can perfect you through." After all, God is first interested in your character (who you really are inside) before revealing your task (what you will do and who you will become). So He blends the three building blocks of manhood—adventure, character, and task—together perfectly just for you according to His perfect plan.

For too many years I thought that the Christian life was all about reading my Bible, praying, going to church, and following certain rules. I drew this conclusion because my mentors were trying to help me develop important spiritual disciplines. But what I failed to understand was that I need a personal relationship with Jesus. I think everyone figured if I just did these things the relationship part would also kick in at some point.

Had I accepted Jesus as my Savior? Yes, of course. But I treated it like a box I'd checked off on a long list of things I needed to do to please God. Slowly, I figured out that what He wants is relationship that grows out of faith in Him. He wants me to trust and follow Him. As I did, I developed a greater hunger for the Word, and I wanted to spend more time with Him. I discovered I could have as personal a relationship with God as the people in the Bible did. It is a close, conversational, and fun relationship with God in the same way I have relationships with family and friends.

So here's my advice—take the long view and look at the big picture, if you will. God is alive. He's fun and has lots of personality. If you look for it, you'll even find Him to be playful. He likes to make you smile and even laugh. He's that close, real, and personal. Look at every call to obey Him as an invitation to adventure, every hardship as a battle that will make you stronger and draw you closer to Him, and every opportunity to serve others as a way to learn about yourself and what makes you come alive.

So what comes first? The chicken or the egg? Yes! So what comes first? Spiritual disciplines like reading the Bible, prayer, and attending church or adventure, character, and task? Yes! The point is, love Jesus and let Him love you. Spend time with Him. Let Him bring you to life. That's the opposite of religious obligation and duty. His invitation to follow is to enter an alive and personal relationship with the God of the universe. That's how God will build you into a real man.

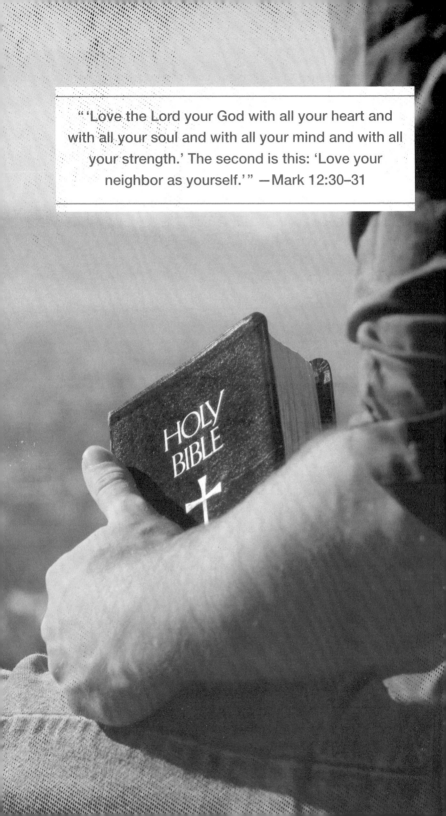

" 'Love the Lord your God with all your heart and with all your soul and with all your mind and with all your strength.' The second is this: 'Love your neighbor as yourself.' " —Mark 12:30–31

myAdventure, hisCommand

Every opportunity to obey God's Word and His instructions is an invitation to adventure

Adventure is always exciting. It's like a magnet that pulls young men, drawing us toward the unknown and unseen. When people ask, "Why did you sled down that steep hill?" we really don't have a logical answer. "I couldn't help it. The hill was there. It was fun." When adventure calls, we answer.

For guys, adventures abound. Exciting activities like shooting bows, creating a movie, or climbing a mountain are all good, wholesome fun, but these are temporary. God intends your entire life to be a spiritual adventure with Him. The kind that makes your palms sweaty, makes your heart race, and makes you shout out in excitement and fear all at once. If your relationship with God doesn't excite you in the same way, it might be because you lack spiritual adventure. In fact, if you're bored in your Christian walk God has the cure—adventure!

Following Jesus Christ is far from boring, except when you play it safe. Mark 8:35 says, "For whoever wants to save their life will lose it, but whoever loses their life for me and for the gospel will save it."

Young men who try to minimize the spiritual adventure God calls them on and to reduce the risks of following His path slowly shrivel and dry up from the inside out. Those who throw themselves into God's plan and follow Him become exceptional men and the leaders God intends them to become.

God calls every Christian into a lifetime of adventure with Him. To be fully alive you must embrace the adventure God calls you on.

God made you for adventure. A ship may be safe at port, but it is not intended to stay in the harbor. A ship is made to explore the wide expanse of the seas, and so are you. You were created to relate with God. He is calling you into the wild. To adventure with God is to really live. Adventure is calling. Life is calling. Answer Him!

CHAPTER 3

From Shepherd to King

In the Old Testament, King David was an amazing man whose life was an adventure. God took this shepherd boy and made him the king of a nation.

As the youngest of his brothers, he was given the unwanted, boring, and occasionally dangerous task of tending sheep. David used his time to talk with God, make music, and write. His main job was to protect the flocks. He fought and killed a bear and a lion that were attacking the sheep. How did a young man defeat these mighty beasts? He had God's strength and wisdom. During the easy times, he was walking and talking with God, and when trouble struck, he was strong and ready.

This is a great life lesson about adventure. The most important decisions you will ever make are your pre-decisions. Before you make big decisions under pressure (like deciding whether to run away or attack and kill a lion), you make them calmly and firmly in advance. You prepare so you are ready for anything, instinctively ready to spring into action. Your spiritual adventures with God, like all great adventures, are preceded by planning. Then when tough decisions come, you will make the right choices.

What kind of pre-decisions do you need to make? Here are some you might think about:

- I will honor God first, above and before anything or anyone else, period!

- I will treat people right in every circumstance.

- I will be a positive influence on my peers, and I won't be swept under by negative peer pressure.

- I will take care of my physical well-being and personal hygiene.

- I will do my best in school.

King David made good pre-decisions, and he had some amazing adventures with God. He started as a shepherd and later became a brave, young warrior, who killed an almost ten-foot tall, previously undefeated giant named Goliath. He then had the honor of serving in King Saul's court and became a high-ranking military officer.

He assembled and led a band of warriors who later became known as David's Mighty Men. He developed relationships of integrity with men, such as his best friend, Jonathan. He was a passionate husband, had kids, and became a poet and songwriter. He became king and achieved many exploits with God's help. David was not perfect, but his whole life was full of spiritual adventures with God.

His was not a life of boredom. In the Bible, God describes King David as "a man after my own heart; he will do everything I want him to do" (Acts 13:22). Nice compliment, right? You bet! Especially considering it came straight from God, who celebrates men who adventure with Him. David's secret to success was that he pre-decided to always do exactly what God wanted him to do— nothing less, nothing more, and nothing else.

When you make a pre-decision to do everything God says without reservation, your adventure will prove successful.

Going on spiritual adventure with God is not optional. It's not like a birthday party invitation. "I might go. I might not. It depends how I feel." God doesn't need the adventure. He's whole and complete, lacking nothing. The adventure is for your good, not His. That's why God invites you to follow Him wholeheartedly.

In Your Own Words:

1. What is the definition of *adventure*?

2. Are you prepared to make a firm pre-decision to do everything God's Word asks? Will you do whatever He instructs you to do? Why or why not?

3. What pre-decisions do you need to make? Can you share them?

In My Experience:

As a young man growing up in Bolivia, pornography was relatively easy for a guy to get his hands on, regardless of age. I made a firm pre-decision not to partake. But that choice was challenged many times.

Once I sat down in the barber's chair and was promptly offered a girly magazine (a common practice by barbers at the time, but seldom, if ever, was it offered to teenagers like me). I refused it. I sat in silence wondering what the barber was thinking. *Does he think less of me as a man?* I didn't have to wait long to find out. He told me, "I know who you are. You're the guy teaching those boys at the Upper Room Church. I wanted to see if you were the real deal." I was so glad I had not caved.

Another time I was feeling very tempted to give in. With my hormones in overdrive and with an intense curiosity fueling my imagination, I found myself at a sidewalk newsstand early one Sunday morning while heading to church. Standing there I was tempted to buy one of the magazines staring me in the face. *This lady selling these magazines and newspapers won't remember me. I'm alone, too. Few people are out this early.* In that moment I called out to God for help. Then something took place that never happens. The bus I was waiting for arrived early. God created a way of escape for me.

Pre-decisions helped me avoid places and people I knew would lead me to a wrong turn. Pre-decisions helped me fight when tempted. They also kept me accountable, because I shared my pre-decisions with friends and mentors. What pre-decisions do you need to make? Who will you share them with? How will you hold yourself accountable?

The Antidote to Spiritual Boredom

God never intended for your spiritual life to be boring. In fact, He intended quite the opposite. Your spiritual journey should be an active, lifetime quest. Your life should be full of fun, exploration, friends, growth, and even hardships that test and prove your strength. That is very different from just playing it safe, anchored to the couch. God shapes strong men as they go on adventure. It's the perfect antidote to spiritual boredom.

God Reveals Himself *ON* Adventure

Yes, you can and must learn about God intellectually from sitting down to read and reflect on His Word, attending church, and participating in devotions and Bible studies. Through the Bible, we learn about God's character, His feelings toward people, and His work patterns and principles. But knowing them and personally experiencing them are two different things. Important learning takes place during disciplined study, but the adventure only starts when you apply what you have learned.

Your beliefs are not revealed by what you say you believe; they are revealed by what you practice, by your daily choices. When you read about God in the Bible, you learn what God says about himself. When you put what you have learned into practice, God will make himself personal to you. He will always come through for you and make the truths of the Bible real in your life. Practicing what you learn in the Bible is when real relationship begins, and there is no adventure like it.

In Luke 19, we read about three men who were given money to invest. The first two men took risks and doubled their employer's investment. This made him very happy, of course, and he rewarded them with big career promotions. Unfortunately, the third guy buried the money he was given; he didn't even put it in the bank to earn interest. He played it safe, which angered his employer. To justify himself, he said, "I was afraid of you, because you are a hard man" (Luke 19:21).

Yes, God reveals himself to you on adventure, but adventure also reveals what you think and feel about God. The third employee had a low opinion of his employer, and that is why he played it safe. If you play it safe spiritually, it may reveal your lack of trust in God. Will God really come through for me if I stand up and get counted as a Christian in my school? Will my witness really influence my peers to also serve Christ? Should I just blend in and hide the fact I'm a Christian?

> For whoever wants to save their life will lose it, but whoever loses their life for me and for the gospel will save it.
> —Mark 8:35

You will never know the answer to these questions until you fully throw yourself into the things of God. Until you risk and "lose your life," your own identity, and become fully identified with Christ, you will not find full life. God reveals himself through adventure.

Choosing a life of adventure with God is not easy. The only way to counter your fears is to let go, trust God, and jump into your adventure with Him. He will absolutely and most certainly come through for you. You won't believe it until you test it, practice it, and discover it yourself. That's why you need adventure.

God Shapes Your Character *ON* Adventure

The lyrics of an old church chorus read, "Change my heart Oh God. Make it ever true. Change my heart Oh God. May I be like You." * There is an inner desire on the part of every one of us to be like Christ. Of course, there is also a desire to live life "my way." In fact, that is what sin is—living life your way instead of God's way (James 4:17). The tug-of-war that every person fights is the desire to please God versus the desire to please self (Romans 7:15,19). This old chorus emphasizes that deep desire in every Christian to live God's way instead of their own way.

It is important to wholeheartedly enter into times of worship and praise at church functions and in personal times of prayer. Singing and praying will deepen your commitment to the Christ-honoring pre-decisions you have made, and at times, they will reveal the need to make other pre-decisions. God does not often change you as you sing and pray. But He will always use those times to prepare you for the adventures ahead, which often include battles that would be lost except for the strength discovered in times of worship and prayer.

The changes He wants to make in your life come most often on your adventure with God. The admirable, manly, and tough Old Testament prophet Isaiah put it this way: "Even youths grow tired and weary, and young men stumble and fall; but those who hope in the LORD will renew their strength. They will soar on wings like eagles; they will run and not grow weary, they will walk and not be faint" (Isaiah 40:30–31).

For example, you can pray, "God make me more generous." But until you start giving away your time and money selflessly for the benefit of others, you will remain unchanged. The adventure might start small by giving your tithe or a missions offering or by

---

* "Change My Heart Oh God" by Eddie Espinosa, 1982, 1987 Mercy Publishing/ Vineyard Music. Used by permission.

volunteering some time to a ministry in your church. Once you take the first step to start an adventure with God, your heart begins to change. When you give, your heart reflects the heart of God, and your heart will grow bigger and stronger. The fists that once clinched and hoarded will begin to loosen their grip on your money and time. You will look at others differently and will reflect God's generous nature toward them. None of that change would happen except for adventure preceded by time with God.

Whenever God calls, go on an adventure with Him. There He will change you to reflect His character.

God Rewards You *AFTER* Adventure

Remember the three guys from Luke 19 who were asked to invest money for their employer? The one who avoided all risk and refused the challenging adventure was severely punished. But the two who braved the chance of failure succeeded. They risked it all for their employer and were rewarded with prestigious promotions. Your life of adventure with God will be rewarded!

The author of Hebrews said, "Without faith it is impossible to please God, because anyone who comes to him must believe that he exists and that he rewards those who earnestly seek him" (Hebrews 11:6). To be sure, every adventure He calls you on will require faith, which is a total trust that He will never let you down or leave you behind. The verse finishes with a great promise. If you go on God's adventure, you will be following Him and depending on Him. He will be your Guide. That is what seeking Him is all about. When you do that, you will be rewarded.

If you accept the call to adventure with God, you can expect rewards. Without going on an all-out faith adventure with God, you can expect church to be dull, the Bible to be a list of rules, and your faith to be dead. If you accept this kind of lifestyle, the best you can expect is microwave popcorn, snuggly blankets, knit sweaters, and flannel pajamas. Skip that! God is calling you into the wild unknown with Him. Follow!

God's adventures are amazing, and His rewards are awesome. Taking risks with God increases your faith, which leads to bigger and better adventures. Your spiritual strength grows. You gain a deep, abiding joy that will see you through tough times. You gain a level of understanding and wisdom beyond your years. Most importantly, your close relationship with God becomes much more intimate. You read the Word differently. You relate with the characters of the Bible because you experience God the way many of them did. God is not a deity you read about in a book; He's a Person involved in your daily life. You read seeking your next adventure, "What is God asking me to obey next?" These rewards last as long as you keep adventuring with God.

God rewards those who adventure with Him. No adventure? No reward! It's that simple.

In Your Own Words:

1. Describe the adventures you have allowed God to take you on lately. Think about those you've shrunk back from. How did your attitude toward God influence your choice of adventures to take or step back from?

2. In what ways has God shaped your life and character when you have accepted His invitation to adventure with Him?

3. Describe the benefits of adventuring with God that you have noticed in your life. If you can't think of any, what does that say about the adventures you are on? Perhaps you are in the middle of an adventure. Are you in tough times and it doesn't feel like an adventure? Do you need to be reminded to keep moving forward?

In My Experience:

I have to admit that some of my adventures start with great expectation but soon feel like a test of endurance. "I'm going to obey God and great things are going to happen!" Soon my words of faith turn to complaining. "Where's God in all this?"

One of the fun activities I most enjoyed about growing up in Bolivia was hiking in the Andes Mountains. My home was at 11,500 feet above sea level and the mountains around La Paz jetted up another 10,000 to 12,000 feet. Living at the foothills of such beauty demanded that I explore it often, and explore it I did.

The ancient Inca civilization established an elaborate road system throughout their empire that my friends and I would hike on weekends and vacations. The Inca trails are extensive and hundreds of miles of it remain intact to this day. My friends and I would anticipate our adventures. We'd ride in the back of open trucks atop cargo on dusty mountain roads to reach a trailhead; often near an abandoned mine. We'd walk on trails where *casiquis* (Inca messengers) had run thousands of years earlier, carrying official mail to or from the emperor in their capital of Cuzco. We'd camp near or in their *tempus* (shelters). We'd look for and avoid witch doctors at high mountain passes. Whenever possible we'd hire llamas to carry our gear. And the views, well, they were just breathtaking. How cool!

But things seldom go as planned. Our poor quality gear, most often our stove, would fail. The tree line is 10,500 feet, so there's little or no wood anywhere. We'd be forced to cook with animal dung. Then it would rain. Or worse, it would mist nonstop, which was the only thing I disliked more than a hard, cold, high-mountain rain. Then there were the river crossings after the rain took out the old rickety footbridge. The swift, turbulent waters were freezing which only added to the danger. Altitude sickness would strike, or someone would sprain an ankle. A promising adventure had gone wrong.

Or had it? I learned that unexpected and unwanted turn-of-events were part of the adventure, not an interruption. I learned the value of preplanning, making "what-if" plans, obtaining or making reliable gear, preparing for emergencies, and most important, pre-determining my attitude.

I know we're talking about a hiking trip here, but all of this is true of adventuring with God as well. Consistently reading your Bible might feel more like a rainstorm than showers of blessings. The missions trip that promised such benefit is stalled out in fund-raising and feels like an impossible uphill climb.

"Where's God in all this?" I asked myself that once. He immediately answered, "Why don't you ask Me?" What a novel thought! Rather than view Him as a distant third party out there somewhere who's abandoned me while out on an adventure, maybe I'd do well to remember He's in me. He's just waiting, like the gentleman He is, to be invited into my situation so we can find a way through it together.

"LOVE THE LORD YOUR GOD."

Mark 12:30

CHAPTER 5

The Great Commandment

J esus gave His followers a command. In fact, He said it is the greatest and most important of all His commands. So we call it the Great Commandment.

Anytime God's Word asks you to do something, it is an invitation to go on an adventure with Him. The Great Commandment is such an invitation. It will never expire. You will never reach its end in your lifetime. This is the greatest adventure because it is a lifelong quest. It is the adventure that all adventures depend on. If you commit to this adventure, you will find the motivation and the strength to undertake all the rest. See how important this is?

So here it is. Jesus' Great Commandment calls you to do two things: (1) to love God with all your mind, with all your heart, and with

The Great Commandment: If you commit to this adventure, you will find the motivation and the strength to undertake all the rest.

all your strength, and (2) to love those around you as much as you love yourself (Mark 12:30–31).

" 'Love the Lord your God with all your heart and with all your soul* and with all your mind and with all your strength.' The second is this: 'Love your neighbor as yourself.' There is no commandment greater than these."
— Mark 12:30–31

If Jesus said this is the greatest and most important commandment, then we should do everything in our power to be great at obeying it. Not just good. Great!

- You love God with all your mind when you respect Him with clean thinking, when you seek Him with curiosity, and when you creatively show the world His care and concern.

- You love God with all your heart when you give Him your passion and interest, when you take the risk of adventuring with Him, and when you overcome your fear of what others think of you for being sold out to Jesus Christ.

- You love God with all your strength when you serve Him with boundless energy and when you make following Him your first priority every day.

- You love people well when you become less self-centered and more others-centered. What can you do to help others today? Who can you encourage today? How can you help others feel like winners today? Focus on meeting the needs of others with integrity and kindness.

You must love God with all three parts of your life, not just one or two. Love Him with all your mind, heart, and strength. When

---

* The "soul" is the seat of intellect, will, and emotion. It is the bridge between "heart" and "mind." Loving God with our whole soul is the sum total of loving God with head, heart, and strength.

you love Jesus fully with all three, your life's adventures will have direction and meaning.

- If you learn about God with your intellect but never adventure with Him or if you fail to regularly enter into passionate worship and prayer, you will know about Him but feel distant from Him.

- If you worship God passionately with your heart but never go out and use your strength to serve others, you might feel close to Him, but others won't know it or be inspired by it.

- If you accomplish great things for God with your strength but know little about Him and seldom seek Him, people will be grateful for your acts of kindness but never detect any true knowledge and passion for God.

Picking and choosing how to love God will leave you running on fumes and will do little to inspire those around you to follow Christ. So the adventure is to love God with all your mind, with all your passion, and with all your physical strength. Choose all three and refuse to be just okay at them. Be great!

To love is to give yourself away. The greatest adventure in life is to love God and to love people. You can give without loving, but you can't love without giving. God loved you so much that He gave His one and only Son, Jesus Christ, at His own expense to die on the cross for your sins. In response to His love, you should give yourself to Him fully.

> *Love* is giving to others at your expense. *Lust* is getting from others at their expense.

The greatest adventure that will undergird all other adventures you undertake is the Great Commandment. By giving yourself to God with all your intellect, with all your passion, and with all your strength, and by giving yourself to others, you discover real meaning. True joy and happiness are found on the giving end of life, not on the getting end. Love God, love people, love life!

In Your Own Words:

1. Can you recite the Great Commandment from memory? If not, take time to memorize Mark 12:30–31.

2. For a moment, think of loving God with all your *mind*, *heart*, and *strength* as three separate levers that control your life. When the three are being used equally, you are in balance. How well-balanced is your love for God?

In My Experience:

Can I make a confession? I didn't discover the need to evenly balance my love for God until more recently, and I regret it. To be frank, I had bought into the lie that the passion, or heart piece, was too emotional for a guy like me. So I emphasized my intellect and service.

My love for God—mind, heart, and strength—was not equally balanced and I felt like a candle about to flicker out. If fire is to provide light, warmth, and create atmosphere, it must have three elements—fuel, oxygen, and heat. If one is missing there is no fire. I was gasping for air and didn't know why.

I found myself studying the Bible as if it were a textbook, as if God were a subject to be mastered. I was dutifully working for Him rather than lovingly serving Him. I acted as if He couldn't accomplish everything I'm doing through someone else or with no one's help at all. I convinced myself that the passion piece was covered simply by the fact I'm Pentecostal, and I didn't want to be one who is "way out there."

But deep inside I knew my zeal was weak. The light came on when I simply ran out of physical and spiritual energy. And believe me when I say the Lord has a sense of humor. I attended a non-Pentecostal church service and saw people passionately in love with Jesus and it showed. I humbled myself and asked God to teach me to love Him from my heart with the same intensity of my head and hands.

The quest to love God from my heart started with an acknowledgement that raising my hands, kneeling in prayer, singing out, lifting my voice to pray were biblical mandates and not optional church traditions. To adventure with God, by doing everything His Word invites me to experience, I was going to have to put myself out there and just do it.

Yes, it was awkward, especially at first. But to start an adventure you have to act your way into obedience and let the feelings catch up later. And that's what happened. The Lord began to teach me to let Him carry me away in His presence, without letting myself get carried away—you know, "worshipping" just to impress someone like a girl, a parent, or a church leader—or doing things just to draw attention to myself.

In the process, my confidence in God and our relationship grew. I did less and less out of fear or a sense of duty and more and more out of love and devotion. I discovered lightness in our relationship, as though the burden of study and service had been lifted. I was still reading the Bible and working as hard as always but felt plugged into the strength of the very One I was studying and working so hard for. My physical and spiritual strength were continually being renewed. Duty turned to joy.

If you commit to being great at the Great Commandment, you will find the motivation and the strength to undertake every adventure God calls you on.

CHAPTER 6

Common and Custom Adventures

The Great Commandment is the adventure that starts them all, but there are many adventures God has for your life. These adventures fall into two categories: (1) the common adventures, the ones God invites everyone to take, and (2) the custom adventures, the ones God tailors just for you.

Here's the deal. God wants to take you on custom adventures. You can be sure of that! You can't expect to enjoy God's custom adventures, however, until you have learned to obey His call into the common adventures.

Common Adventures

A common adventure is like the Great Commandment. Jesus' call for us to love Him and to love people is an adventure for everyone. Don't think of common adventures as less significant than a custom one. They are like the foundation to a home. No matter how awesome a home is, without a strong foundation the house is unstable.

In Matthew 7:24–27, Jesus told a big crowd that a person who adventures with Him by learning His Word and doing it was like a wise man who built his house on a solid foundation. The storms of life came, and that man stood strong. Jesus compared that to a person whose life was not build on obedience to God's Word, a person whose life was not characterized by accepting God's call to adventure with Him. That person had a poor foundation, and when the storms of life came, his life crumbled.

Your obedience to the common adventures will ensure your life has a strong and sturdy foundation that will last. Here's a short list of the adventures God calls everyone on:

- Be great at living the Great Commandment to love God with all your mind, with all your heart, and with all your strength, and to love people by giving to them at your own expense.

- Soon after making a firm personal commitment to follow Christ as your Friend and the only Leader of your life, show that in a public way by being baptized in water.

- Show God that you trust and honor Him to provide for all your needs by giving Him the first 10 percent of the money you earn or receive and living on the 90 percent that's left.

- Let God strengthen your character by depending completely on His Holy Spirit to power your life with the baptism in the Holy Spirit, the fruit of the Spirit, and the gifts of the Spirit.

- Become God's ally in this world, syncing up your dreams and interests with God's everlasting purposes.

The best part of these adventures is that they are not burdensome duties. They are intentionally big and challenging. These adventures can be scary and may be difficult at times. But after you start them, you begin to see what your faith and trust in God can do. When you enter these adventures with God, He starts to make changes in you that He cannot make any other way. Until you start

Real Life Adventures:

Talk with your pastors, parents, or mentors and ask them about people they know that live these adventures and how it has shaped their lives, and how these have shaped their own lives. Write some of these in the space below:

and stick with these, you won't understand. So go ahead, test it. Say good-bye to boring spirituality. God will supernaturally shape your life, and you will never feel more alive!

Custom Adventures

As you begin to grow in your adventures with God, He will call you into some unique situations. Sometimes, these adventures develop into careers like becoming bankers, politicians, salesmen, teachers, missionaries, pastors, evangelists, pilots, manufacturers, builders, architects, artists, actors, musicians, and too many others to name. As you follow Him in the common adventures, several events happen to prepare you for the custom adventures.

- You learn to trust God. When He starts to lead you into these new adventures, you are ready to follow.

- You start to learn about yourself. You discover your strengths. God brings people into your life to help you.

- God slowly shapes you into His likeness, to be like Him. He gives you a new heart, transforms your mind and thinking, and conforms your will to His own.

- God starts to reward your faith and your confidence matures.

- God learns He can trust you. This is big! You see, God does His greatest exploits through men He can trust. So be faithful in all your adventures with God!

There is no simple way to describe God's custom adventures because no two are alike. God loves to be God. He loves to lead us. He loves to do good works in our lives. You can trust Him. Start with the common adventures and hold on because the custom adventures are awesome!

In Your Own Words:

1. In your own words describe the difference between a common and a custom adventure. Can you recall examples of each from the lives of Bible characters?

2. Tell some of the common adventures you have followed God on. How about some of the custom adventures? Can you share examples from people you know and admire?

In My Experience:

Obedience has a compounding effect. That means if you do the right thing today and tomorrow and the next day, for a long time, then together, the small acts of kindness, honesty, courage, risk, and loyalty have a combined effect greater than you ever thought possible. It's like a snowball rolling down a hill that starts small and slow and gets bigger and faster the further it rolls.

When I started my first Royal Rangers group in La Paz, Bolivia, as a thirteen-year-old, I was scared to death. But God was taking me on a custom adventure because I'd been faithful to follow Him on the common ones. Little did I know my obedience would make it possible to start a total of thirty-three groups before graduating from high school, to travel all over Latin America and the Caribbean training leaders to mentor next generation men while attending college, to become a missionary, and to become the international and later the national director of Royal Rangers. I've ministered all over the United States and in over seventy nations around the world. I am so glad I heard God's call!

Adventuring with God has a multiplying effect in your life. Doing what's right increases your personal confidence. People trust you because they know they can count on you. It opens doors. Nothing will have a greater compounding effect in your life than committing yourself to do everything God invites you to do.

"THE ONE WHO IS WISE SAVES LIVES."

Proverbs 11:30

Invitation to Adventure

Adventuring with others is better than alone. So invite others to go with you. If you don't have many saved friends, win some over! This is a big part of the great adventure God has for you.

Through the years, people have come up with varied and simple ways to tell others about Jesus. Don't get hung up on using the method perfectly. They are just guides; the Holy Spirit is the Ultimate Guide. Rely on Him, not the method. He will help you tell your friends about Christ.

Here are three great ways to help you lead someone to Christ. If you want to make a difference in your friends' lives, commit one of these to memory and begin to use it.

The ABCs of Salvation

This is a method that is commonly used to clearly present the gospel. ABC is an acronym for the following (the "C" can represent one of two things):

A—Admit	Admit you are a sinner in need of a Savior.
B—Believe	Believe that Jesus is the Son of God and that God raised Him from the dead.
C—Confess or C—Commit	Confess your sins and that Jesus Christ is Lord. Commit your life to following Jesus.

The Romans Road

Some people prefer to use the Scriptures to explain the plan of salvation. In doing so, they use a method called, "The Romans Road." It comes from two verses: Romans 3:23 and 6:23.

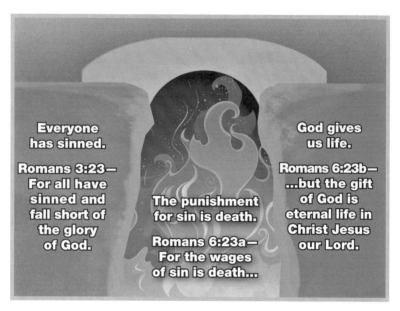

Everyone has sinned.

Romans 3:23—For all have sinned and fall short of the glory of God.

The punishment for sin is death.

Romans 6:23a—For the wages of sin is death...

God gives us life.

Romans 6:23b—...but the gift of God is eternal life in Christ Jesus our Lord.

The Salvation Poem

The Salvation Poem was written by Matt and Sherry McPherson. Matt grew up in the church and in Royal Rangers. Today, he is a successful entrepreneur and inventor. His greatest passion is guiding people to become followers of Christ. He and his wife arranged salvation Scriptures into a poem that is as easy to remember as a nursery rhyme.

Visit www.thesalvationpoem.com where you will find the poem has also been turned into a song and a music video.

Telling your friends what Jesus has done for them is quite an adventure—it requires that your words and actions match. They don't want to just hear about adventures in following God, they need to see yours. You have to do your part, but it is ultimately the

Holy Spirit who is doing the supernatural job and changing their heart from the inside out.

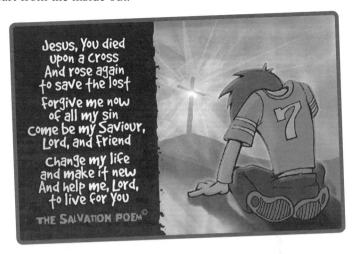

The Salvation Poem	Selected Scriptures
Jesus, You died upon a cross	Romans 5:8—But God demonstrates his own love for us in this: While we were still sinners, Christ died for us.
And rose again to save the lost	John 3:16—For God so loved the world that he gave his one and only Son, that whoever believes in him shall not perish but have eternal life.
Forgive me now of all my sin	1 John 1:9—If we confess our sins, he is faithful and just and will forgive us our sins and purify us from all unrighteousness.
Come be my Savior, Lord, and Friend	Romans 10:9—If you declare with your mouth, "Jesus is Lord," and believe in your heart that God raised him from the dead, you will be saved.
Change my life and make it new	2 Corinthians 5:17—If anyone is in Christ, the new creation has come: The old has gone, the new is here!
And help me, Lord, to live for You.	Colossians 2:6—Just as you received Christ Jesus as Lord, continue to live your lives in him.

Ready yourself by becoming acquainted with a method you are comfortable with. Then memorize key Scriptures. God's Word builds faith in Christ. Also, reflect on what God's grace has accomplished in your life. Walk the walk and then talk the talk by telling your own story, weaving in key verses. Then, as you tell your friends about Jesus in word and deed, pray for them, that the Holy Spirit will perform the miracle of salvation as He convinces them to put their trust in God through Jesus.

There is no greater adventure than inviting your friends to faith in Christ. Help your friends start their own adventure with God.

Bow, Guitar, and Poem: Matt McPherson

When Matt McPherson was a young man, God set him on an adventure to reach people who weren't in relationship with Jesus Christ. However, the talents and skills Matt embodied led him to pursue this passion for the lost in a very different way, a custom adventure for sure.

Early on, Matt realized the crucial role finances play in the success of a ministry. Many times ministry concepts and ideas fail due to inadequate financial support. In 1992, Matt started his own bow manufacturing company, Mathews, Inc., with a core objective of supporting the work of ministry. He committed to honor God in all he did, and God blessed his business. It became one of the fastest growing companies in America, earned the distinction of *Inc. Magazine's* top 500 companies two years in a row, and received over twenty patents.

With all of his business accomplishments, Matt continues to consider his personal relationship with Christ his highest priority. "I came to Christ at a very early age," Matt declares. "My father was a pastor, and my mother would have devotions every night with us kids. She would pray with us. I realized at a very early age that Christ and the Bible made sense to me, and I began to ask God to help me to find ways to reach others for Him."

With all of his business accomplishments, Matt McPherson considers his personal relationship with Christ his highest priority.

Matt credits his success at Mathews, Inc. completely to God. "I learned early to depend on God for everything and that keeping God in the center of my business would be my first priority. I have to admit there were times when things got tough and we were nervous. We would have hundreds of thousands of dollars in invoices coming due, and it wasn't clear how we were going to pay them. But time and again, we would pray for God's wisdom, asking Him for help with our finances and for guidance in making a better product to better serve our customers. He always came through for us."

After the success of Mathews, Inc., Matt turned his attention to his long-standing love for music and started making his own unique style of guitar. "I started redesigning a guitar in the late 1990s. Again, I got on my knees and began to ask God for wisdom and direction to make a better guitar, something really unique."

The McPherson guitar is indeed unique in both sound and style. Now, this finely crafted instrument has become a hit with music professionals like Steven Curtis Chapman, Tim Hawkins, and Chris Tomlin.

Matt's success in bow- and guitar-making has enabled him to provide substantial support to ministries across the nation and around the world. "We're typically involved with ministries that focus on evangelism and give people the opportunity to come to Christ. I believe that's ultimately the most important role of any ministry, and it's the role I'm most passionate about."

One of Matt's favorite accomplishments is the creation of the Salvation Poem. This simple, easy-to-remember poem represents an individual's personal commitment to Christ. The poem has also been recorded as a song and is publicly broadcast in both English and Spanish.

Through it all, Matt continues to give God the credit for all his successes. "It's clear to me that God has been part of this adventure from the beginning. There is simply no way I could have accomplished all these things without His direction."

Matt also acknowledges the influence of godly mentors in a boys program for shaping his faith and commitment to God. "Royal Rangers was a bright spot in my life. I remember the awesome feeling of being a part of something big, something greater than ourselves or our small group," says Matt. The time his mentor, Dennis, invested in his life helped him learn to pray, share Christ, and become a strong Christian man. "It was really a pivotal time in my life."

Matt McPherson is an excellent example of a young man who learned from mentors to accept God's every call, to adventure with Him. To this day Matt continues to follow the Lord, invest in others, and influence his world with his unique gifts.

"You will receive power when the Holy Spirit comes on you." —Acts 1:8

myCharacter, hisPower

Every battle* you face is God's opportunity to strengthen your character in His power.

Men are created by God to defend the weak and provide for those under our care.

An old movie trailer ends with these words: "The lives of many rest in the courage of a few." In the battle, a small band of warriors rescues a doctor from a remote African jungle, along with the villagers she was caring for, before rebel forces overtake the province. The lives of these defenseless people depended entirely on the strength and determination of these brave fighting men.

This is a picture of Jesus' courage. He was willingly executed on a cross but rose to life to set you free from the chains and limitations sin places on your life and from its destruction of dreams, potential, and future. One Man died for all humanity to make an off-ramp from the dead-end road of sinful living. He died so you could be free, so you could be a winner, so you could be your best, so you could become a man of God, and so you could live with Him for eternity in heaven. The only action required from you is to submit

*every choice, challenge, and temptation; all the losses and wins; your successes and failures

yourself to Him and follow Him. As you do, He will make you strong like He is.

You will need all of God's strength because you and I were born into a real battle. Life is for keeps and we have an enemy: Satan. He is not using rubber bullets. He's out to destroy you because it is the only way he can get back at God. God loves you, and Satan can't touch God; therefore, he goes after you because you are the object of God's love, concern, and respect. By attacking you, he's attacking God. But that's why God gave you a warrior's heart like His own. Take it seriously and learn to fight with all of God's power so you can grow strong without getting taken out!

John 16:33 should encourage you: "In this world you will have trouble. But take heart! I have overcome the world." Jesus has already won the war. When you do battle, you are taking hold of things Jesus has already won for you by His death and resurrection. It is your right as a chosen child of God to have every good thing He intends for you. But it won't be handed to you on a silver platter. You'll have to fight for it because you have an enemy who wants to deny you what God has planned. In the future, when we are in heaven and God has set all things right, everything will come easy to you. But for now, take courage and fight because Jesus has overcome the world. The battles you face are shaping you into the courageous man God created you to become!

Your life, and the lives of many others, rest in your courage!

CHAPTER 7

The Warrior Within

"The lives of many rest in the courage of a few." There is something about this statement that resonates in the heart of a young man. We all want to be significant the same way Jesus was. We want to free people, to protect them, to be a hero. We want to come through for ourselves and on behalf of others. And that is what God wants for you, too. God wants men to be strong inside and out to help others, freeing them the way He frees us from our sins.

"It is for freedom that Christ has set us free." —Galatians 5:1

But where does that desire to stand and fight come from? Would you believe it comes from God himself? Did you know that God describes himself as a warrior? It's true! Check this out:

- Exodus 15:3—"The LORD is a warrior, the LORD is his name."

- Psalm 24:8—"Who is this King of glory? The LORD strong and mighty, the LORD mighty in battle."

- Jeremiah 20:11—"The LORD is with me like a mighty warrior."

So the heart you have to compete and to win in life is from God, and it is good. To live successfully, you will need this fighting heart. Life is full of obstacles from all sides. Unless you are willing to confront them courageously, you'll get taken out. If you are prepared to fight for what is good and wholesome, God will prepare you to win and overcome. As you gain strength from victories and courage to fight again after defeat, God will build you into an overcoming warrior who has what it takes to live strong and share your strength with others.

A Human Target

You have an enemy. He is Satan. He wants to trip you up at every turn. He wants to attack you in every way possible. Satan has a bull's eye on your back.

Peter, one of Jesus' disciples, wrote a letter to fellow Christians and said, "Be alert and of sober mind." In other words, don't be fooled into having a dismissive attitude. Be on your guard! You have an enemy out to get you. Peter continues in his letter, "Your enemy the devil prowls around like a roaring lion looking for someone to devour" (1 Peter 5:8). Lions don't make good house pets. If you think back on the programs you've watched about wild African beasts, you know that lions maim and kill their prey. That is Satan's purpose. He's not your house pet; he's your enemy!

Peter is echoing Jesus' words and wants you to know that there is a predator who intends to take you out. Jesus said, "The thief comes only to steal and kill and destroy." The devil has no good intentions toward you, your family, or your friends. He opposes your dreams, your talents, and your future.

But there is good news. Jesus immediately gave us this encouragement when He said, "I have come that they may have life, and have it to the full" (John 10:10). Yes, there is an enemy, but Jesus invites us to enjoy His protection and provision in the battles we face against our enemy. As a warrior you will have to face your enemy often. But you will do it in God's strength and He will be at your side.

Where did Satan come from? Originally, he was an angel created by God, but God had to punish him for trying to make himself greater than God. Ultimately, Satan and his followers will be condemned to eternal punishment. Until then, we must contend with him on earth. Fortunately, we do not contend alone.

C.S. Lewis said we make two mistakes when dealing with devils, including Satan. First, we make a mistake if we "feel an excessive and unhealthy interest in them."* But we also make a mistake when we don't even believe they exist. Both extremes—wanting to know too much about them or not even believing in them—are dangerous. And in our culture today, many people don't even believe Satan exists.

But you have a very real enemy: Satan. He'd love for you to live your life blindly, confused by everything that is set against you. He wants you to blame God for everything going wrong in your life while denying Satan's very existence. But Jesus wants to remove the blinders from your eyes so you can see Him, and so you can gain His strength to do battle and to be victorious.

"Every good and perfect gift is from above, coming down from the Father of the heavenly lights, who does not change like shifting shadows" (James 1:17). Learn it now and learn it well: God's intentions toward you are always good. He wants you to become the very best version of you possible. His plans for you are perfect. But also learn this: Evil stands between you and everything good that God has for you. With God's strength and presence, you will have to fight to take hold of what God has for you.

You have an enemy. You are a warrior. You have the same warrior's heart that God has. When you choose to follow Him, He will teach

---

* C.S. Lewis, *The Screwtape Letters* (New York: HarperCollins Publishers, 1942, 1961, 1996), ix.

you how to battle at His side. He is all-powerful and will share His strength with you to win if you invite Him into all your battles.

God's Got Your Back

God is eternal and infinite. No one created Him, and no one will take Him out. He had no start and will have no end.

God is all-powerful. There is no force equal to His. Not even close. No contest. God will never be defeated, ever. Not by anything or anyone, period.

God knows everything. He loves it when mankind makes break-through discoveries and inventions, but He's never surprised. We can't teach Him things He doesn't already know. In fact, all knowledge comes from Him.

God is present everywhere, always, and at the same time. He's eternally existent. That means that the limitations of time and space don't apply to God. Science fiction stories about time travel and teleportation are everyday occurrences for Him.

God is only limited by His own nature. He will never violate His own Word. For example, God will always be good and never bad. God will always be truthful and never lie. God will always treat you right and never harm you.

God has no equal, no peers. We never have to doubt. God's goodness will triumph over evil. God will totally defeat Satan and his armies at a time of God's choosing. Until then, you must fight for everything good that God intends for you. And you are not alone. God is your Father. He will help you grow strong and teach you how to fight.

In Your Own Words:

1. Can you find examples in the Bible where God fights for His people? Does Jesus ever pick a fight? If so, with whom does He most frequently fight and why?

2. Have you ever thought of yourself as a warrior? Reflecting on Jesus' example, when and how is it appropriate to fight?

3. Read and reflect on these Bible verses: 1 Peter 5:8; John 10:10; 2 Corinthians 4:4; Ephesians 6:12; James 1:17. What are Satan's intentions toward you? How about God's?

4. What are some of the battles you are facing today that you need God's help to win?

In My Experience:

When I was six years old, my family went to the ocean for vacation. It was in a small coastal town in Peru called Mejia. There was a rugged mountain formation that separated two beautiful beaches. There were two ways to cross that rock formation from one beach to another. One was a slow safe route; the other was faster though dangerous.

The slow and safe route was a path over the rocks that took about five to six minutes. The fast and dangerous route was a path through the rock formation directly on the beach, just as soon as the waves went back out to sea. When the water backed out, you had less than thirty seconds to run as fast as you could to the other beach, dodging and jumping over rocks before the waves came crashing in, covering the area with twenty to thirty feet of water.

My parents always insisted that my brother, sister, and I take the safe route. But one day we decided to risk taking the other. My heart was pounding in my chest as all three of us waited for the right moment to dash through the rocks to the other beach. My brother gave the signal and we took off!

The Bible says there is a way that seems right to a man or boy, but in the end it leads to death. As I ran with all my strength through the rocks, I didn't know that I was running through a death trap.

The Bible says we all have to choose between two life paths. One is the safe and long path. The Bible says it is narrow and walked on by only a few, even though it leads to friendship with God and to life eternal. The other way is short and dangerous. The Bible says this path is wide and walked on by many, even though it leads us into Satan's destructive plans and ultimately to eternal death (which is separation from God forever, with no hope of restoring our relationship with Him).

As I ran through those rocks that day, I fell further and further behind my older brother and sister. This scared me. Suddenly I looked at the waves I heard coming in to my right. In a panic, I turned and began running back to where we had started. But when

I noticed the waves were even closer to the rocks in that direction, I turned around again running in the direction of my brother and sister. As I looked how far I had to run and how fast the waves were coming in, I knew I was trapped. Would I die? If so, how? Would I be knocked unconscious on the rocks? Would my lungs explode gasping for oxygen? I didn't know. All I knew is that I had made a terrible choice to disobey my parents and take the short, dangerous path. The only way I'd get out alive is if someone bigger and stronger saved me.

The sooner in life you come to the realization that you are on the wrong path and that you will die in your sin unless Jesus—who is bigger and stronger than your sin—saves you, the better. The thieves on the crosses next to Jesus each realized they had chosen the wrong life path the night they died. One was defiant and said, "I've made a wrong choice, and I'm in this death trap now. But I'll handle it myself." He died and went to hell. The other was humble and said, "I've made a wrong choice. I need Jesus who is bigger and stronger than me to get me on the right path." After that thief accepted Christ into his heart, Jesus said, "Today you'll be with Me in paradise" (Luke 23:32–43).

You see, the Bible says there is no other person you can call on who can save you except Jesus. He is the only One who can save you and me from the death of sin. Why? Jesus died on the cross and rose from the dead to teach you how to live life His right way instead of your wrong way.

As I ran, I watched the waves get closer and closer and I knew I'd soon be overtaken and smashed up against the rocks. Suddenly at the very last second, my brother came running at me, and without slowing down he grabbed me less than a second before a huge wave bowled over me. With me in his arms, he thrust himself into the wave. My brother is seven years older than me and was a strong swimmer, and with great skill he saved my life. That is when I learned how much my brother loves me. He was willing to put his life at risk in an effort to save me from what would have been certain death.

Jesus expressed His love to me and to you in the same way. He died on the cross to save you from the death that sin produces in your life. He rose from the dead to lead you on His path—the right path. He's got your back. Have you given Him your life?

I'm so grateful God spared my life that day. If He hadn't, you would not be holding this book. I would have never met my wife and we would have had no life together. Our kids would have never been born. You and me, we owe everything to God. He breathed life into us, protects us, helps us, and He intends to make us strong and useful as we draw close to Him every day.

CHAPTER 8

Schemes and Tactics

Paul, the great missionary and Early Church planter, wrote, "We are not unaware of his schemes" (2 Corinthians 2:11). Like good soldiers, we must learn how Satan attacks us so we can be ready.

About Satan, Jesus said, "There is no truth in him. When he lies, he speaks his native language, for he is a liar and is the father of lies" (John 8:44). The Bible gives us an intelligence report so we know what we're up against. Satan, the author of lies, uses two primary weapons of deceit to trip us up: accusation and condemnation.

Accusation

Satan's chief weapon against us is accusation. His goal is to create just enough doubt so you will agree with his lie or half-truth. His voice will make accusations against God, against people around you, and against you. For instance:

- Satan will accuse God of holding out on you. Satan deceived Adam and Eve when he told them God didn't want them to eat the fruit because it would make them as smart as Him.

We know, for example, that God wants us to remain virgins until we are married. So Satan will say, "God is holding out on you. He doesn't want you to have fun. He knows sex is pleasurable and won't let you enjoy it." The truth is that God does want you to experience the wonder and beauty of sexual relations. In fact, He invented it for our pleasure. But it isn't just for our pleasure. It is also so we can enjoy a greater degree of intimacy with our wife than with any other person in the world. Sex is a gift to be shared with her and her alone. Intimacy with her allows you to conceive and raise children in the ideal setting of a home with a loving mother and father who are committed to God, each other, and their children for a lifetime together. But the devil won't tell you all that. In fact, he will try to make the very word *virgin* something to be mocked. He's just trying to create enough doubt in God that you'll buy into his lie. When you agree with him, he's got you. And when you act on his lie, you deteriorate the foundations of your life.

- Satan will accuse authority figures in your life of holding out on you too. "If your mom and dad just understood you better, they'd let you do that," Satan might say. All he needs is some agreement, some doubt, and he can nudge your attitude and behaviors off course just enough to change your life path. And that will change your destination to a place you don't ever want to reach. Satan's the mastermind of dead ends.

This is why the Bible places such emphasis on honoring your parents. The godly authority figures in your life usually know what's best and want the best for you. But if Satan can get you to believe the lie that those over you have it in for you, he can create a rebellious spirit that will separate you from those who care about you most. We have seen this from watching nature. What happens to an animal that is alone in the wild? He is an easy kill. Don't let Satan separate you from those who love you and want the best for you when you need them most.

- Satan will accuse you. "You're just faking it. You sinned yesterday, and now you are raising your hands to praise

God? You hypocrite!" Again, all he needs is some self-doubt, some agreement with the lie, and he can misdirect you. It might be true; you might have sinned yesterday. As soon as you realize you have sinned, confess it to the Lord and ask His forgiveness, God will forgive you. Then, when Satan accuses you, just keep on praising the Lord because you know God has forgiven you. Never stop doing what is right just because you made a mistake in the past.

God will never point you in the wrong direction. Satan is a broken compass, but God always shows you the right path. So when you hear a voice, you can determine it is God if the outcome will be wholesome. If the outcome will harm you, it is not God who speaks.

The truth will always benefit you, a lie never will. So if you are tempted, "Go ahead, push the envelope with your girlfriend. She'll like it, and the guys will know you are a man." Stop in that moment and fast-forward to the consequences. In this case, we know that going too far will hurt you, her, and many others. This is clearly not God speaking. Don't agree with Satan's lie! It won't be easy. You'll have to fight back your primal impulses, but you can do it. God's way is good and perfect. Choose His way. When you do, you will discover God never holds out on you. He reserves the best for those who live life His way. Have faith in that fact.

Condemnation

Satan's next big weapon is condemnation. Condemnation is the shame and guilt you feel after sinning. It's that voice that puts you down. There's a very important difference between condemnation and conviction.

Condemnation is the voice of Satan while conviction is the voice of God's Holy Spirit. Conviction is the voice you most often hear before you sin, perhaps while you are being tempted, calling you to choose what is best—what is true, noble, right, pure, lovely, admirable, excellent, or praiseworthy (see Philippians 4:8). When you listen, conviction will give you a battle plan to fight back the temptation and win.

Condemnation, on the other hand, is the voice that comes after you have sinned. The very one who convinced you how fun and harmless the sin is pounces on you after you commit it. Satan is two-faced. Before you sin, Satan's seductive voice urges you to go full throttle, "It will be okay. Your actions won't hurt anyone. No one will ever know. It will feel good." But then, his condemning voice immediately pounds you over and over after the fact, "You're a loser. Everyone knows it, too. You are weak. You'll never amount to anything in God's eyes."

Satan is two-faced: he offers sweets before you sin and shoves sand and gravel down your throat afterwards. (See Proverbs 20:17.)

Many times Satan uses his condemning voice when you have not sinned at all and tries to impersonate the voice of God. "You didn't read your Bible today," he might say, "I'm so disappointed!" See how he tries to cloak his evil voice and make it appear like God is speaking?

Romans 8:1 says, "There is now no condemnation for those who are in Christ Jesus." God does not condemn His sons; He convicts them. Conviction calls you upward; it invites you to choose what is best. In His loving kindness, God invites you to try again and succeed after failing and sinning. Condemnation tears you down with shame and guilt and tries to keep you pinned down. God will never beat you down.

Accusation and condemnation are Satan's dual weapons he wields to trip you up. How do you fight back and win? That's next.

In Your Own Words:

1. Recount times Satan has accused God, authority figures in your life, and you yourself. As you reflect on them, what can you learn?

2. Describe times you heard Satan's voice of condemnation and times you heard God's voice of conviction. Describe times you have mistaken one for the other. Why is it so easy to get them confused? What is the intended purpose of each voice?

In My Experience:

Like most every other boy in human history, I had an eye for spotting pretty girls, at least after I got through the stage of thinking they all had cooties. And, of course, being attracted to the opposite sex is natural and good.

God put a piece of His own beauty in girls—physically and emotionally they reflect His grace, tenderness, and mercy. For that reason few things will capture a guy's attention more quickly. God also put a big chunk of His own drive, strength, and protective instincts into guys, and that's what catches a girl's attention. The two sexes reflect God's beauty. When you notice a girl, you are literally seeing a reflection of God's glory and beauty, and when she notices you, she sees the same.

So what does this have to do with Satan's schemes and tactics? Everything! One of the most common struggles guys face is how to glorify God in their sexuality. You can do what is right. You really can! Our society tells boys and men that faithfulness is not possible, but that's Satan's lie. Young man, from personal experience I can tell you it is possible to remain faithful. On my wedding night, my wife and I exchanged our greatest gift, our virginity. We saved ourselves for that special someone and never regretted it.

But saving that gift for her wasn't easy. As a teen I struggled with my thought life and with lust, and never really learned to distinguish the difference between God's voice of conviction and Satan's voice of condemnation. I interpreted both as God's voice of condemnation, which doesn't exist, but I attributed what Satan was feeding me as God's disapproval.

I begged forgiveness only to fail repeatedly, to feel the shame and guilt over and over. The biggest mistake I made was to keep it silent too long. Satan convinced me my dad would think less of me if he knew, and that God wouldn't accept me until I got it right. So I kept it a secret from both and struggled quietly.

Sin thrives in the darkness of silence but withers in the light of openness. I should have talked with my dad or a godly mentor much sooner than I did. As for God, He knew all along what I was going through and was simply waiting for me to invite Him into it. Once I did, God, my dad, and a close friend helped me. Though it wasn't easy, I discovered I had the inside stuff it takes to please God. And so do you.

Let me close with some advice based on my experience:

- Seek God, not girls. If you do, you'll get God and He'll lead you to the right lady with whom you can share your strength for a lifetime. Don't look for bananas in Alaska—that is, look for a godly girl where they hang out. You can't expect to find her bar hopping. She'll be the one in a life group at church, the one praying at the altar, the one serving others.

- Go for God's stamp of approval on your life and on your manhood. Nothing will honor God more or be as attractive to a girl.

- Save yourself sexually for marriage. Don't even push the boundaries or experiment. You and your wife will have a lifetime to explore together. Protecting your girlfriend's virginity, even if she won't become your wife, is your highest responsibility as a true gentleman. Then, when the day comes for you to teach your children about sex, you'll be able to proudly share your example of purity.

- Avoid pornography like the plague! Even viewing it "casually" can reap terrible results, leading quickly to a life-controlling habit or addiction. Impure sexual thoughts can take over your life. Lust becomes the lens through which you view all your relationships, with a devastating impact on your ability to develop a healthy, godly relationship with that special lady God intends for you. Paul tells the Corinthians, "Flee from sexual immorality. All other sins a person commits are outside the body, but whoever sins sexually, sins against their own body" (1 Corinthians 6:18). Falling into this deadly snare will hurt you personally and those around you. Stay away from porn at all cost!

- Get help if you are struggling. Do it now! If you wait, Satan will get a foothold. He'll sidetrack you from the real treasure, which is God. And he will get you to establish bad habits that you'll spend years breaking. Go to God and to godly men for help and do it until you are free (James 5:16).

There is nothing like offering strength to my wife. My goal is to love her more than God does, which I know isn't possible, but I think trying honors Him nonetheless. I'm glad I didn't compromise when I was a teen. The struggles I faced only made me stronger, especially since I didn't give up. Young man, honoring God is a relief. Honor Him with your youthful strength, and someday, your wife and kids will call themselves blessed because you were wise beyond your years.

> "BE ALERT AND OF SOBER MIND. YOUR ENEMY THE DEVIL PROWLS AROUND LIKE A ROARING LION LOOKING FOR SOMEONE TO DEVOUR."
>
> 1 Peter 5:8

CHAPTER 9

Operational Plans

It might sound impossible to stand up to Satan and win, but you can and you must! Remember, God has already defeated him and will someday soon destroy him; he will be punished for all eternity while you enjoy God's presence in heaven forever and ever. Until then, you have to learn to stand with God and do battle against the enemy of your soul. Here's how to fight alongside God and win.

Stand with God

Apart from a relationship with God, you don't stand a chance.
Satan has been around thousands of years and has become really good at deceiving bright, well-intentioned people into thinking life without God will work just fine. God thinks the world of you; you are the apple of His eye! He already showed

> "Those who honor me I will honor."
> —1 Samuel 2:30

you how much He loved you by creating you and by sending Jesus to die on the cross to pay the penalty for your sin.

But like Adam and Eve, you have to choose friendship with God over friendship with the world. If you do, He will draw you into an amazing adventure. With Him you will win, because God is for you and never against you!

Part of having a relationship with your Heavenly Father means knowing that He will forgive you when you fail. He knew every sin you would ever commit before you were ever born. In spite of that, He was willing to send His Son to die for your sins. That should motivate you to sin less and less. But when you do sin, go to the Father in prayer, and He will forgive you. 1 John 1:9 says, "If we confess our sins, he is faithful and just and will forgive us our sins and purify us from all unrighteousness." Never let Satan's condemnation make you run away and hide from God. Rather, run to Him for forgiveness, healing, and restoration.

God is your friend! Even when we struggle to be free from sin, His kindness helps us to become victorious. Paul wrote to the young preacher, Titus, that God's grace "teaches us to say 'No' to ungodliness and worldly passions, and to live self-controlled, upright and godly lives" (Titus 2:11–12). Again, God is your friend. His kindness and long-suffering help us become strong and able warriors even when we don't feel like it.

Be Alert

Never doubt it! Satan's intentions are to take you out. Satan is subtle, more than you will ever know. There are times Satan shows his hand, and you can tell he is throwing everything he has at you. But more often than not, he wants to nudge you off course in ways you won't recognize. In fact, he wants to camouflage his actions so that you will even begin to doubt he exists. That's another lie he wants you to believe.

Today, Satan's preferred cloaking device is familiarity. Rather than hide, he wants to be seen everywhere —games, movies, clothing, books, stores, and billboards— anywhere really. This tactic lowers your defenses. It portrays him as just another common villain when in reality he's your mortal enemy.

Every good hunter knows the importance of not being seen, heard, smelled, or otherwise noticed. If a buck detects the presence of a hunter, it will snort and speed away while waving its tail in the air, alerting other deer in the area of danger. The hunter has been busted! When a wild African lion successfully takes down a zebra or any other animal for that matter, it is because the lion maintained the advantage of surprise. The poor zebra didn't know the danger

> "Be alert and of sober mind. Your enemy the devil prowls around like a roaring lion looking for someone to devour."
> —1 Peter 5:8

it was in until it was too late. That's the position Satan wants you in. He wants to be totally out of sight or become so familiar that you don't even notice him anymore.

Satan wants your defenses low to make you easy prey. If he can go unnoticed, he might even be able to make you conclude God himself is the cause of all the pain in your life and that God is against you. That makes you defensive toward God and blind toward Satan's actions against you.

So be alert. Don't let your defenses down. Be on the lookout! How is he accusing you? How is he condemning you? Look for it. It's there. Don't let yourself be easy prey.

Know God's Truth

You must become very familiar with God's voice of truth. The only way to recognize a lie is to know the truth. A lie can sound so inviting, but the truth protects you from falling for it. Satan is a very convincing liar. He will even include half-truths to make his lies sound sweet and difficult to detect. If you don't know the truth, it's easy to believe a lie. Everything will sound convincing.

You learn God's voice, the truth, by becoming more and more familiar with His Word. John 10:27 says, "My sheep listen to my voice; I know them, and they follow me." To prevent being deceived by Satan's lies you must know God's voice. He only speaks the truth in love.

The Bible is God's Word. It is true from cover to cover. There are no errors. It is the only foundation on which you can build a solid and good life. It is the standard against which you measure the quality of your behaviors, attitudes, and choices. It is your road map for life. It defines what you should believe about yourself, about others, about God, about Satan, about your life, and about your future.

Our greatest defense against the devil is to learn to hear God's voice in His Word and to do everything He asks. When we do, we build our lives on a foundation that is solid and true, the only one that will never crack or fall apart.

The Secret Service is charged with protecting the president of the United States, other high-ranking governmental leaders, and visiting foreign heads of state. You may not know that they are also responsible for protecting the American currency from counterfeiters. To teach them how to detect fake bills, agents are taught how to identify quickly and easily a real bill. When they know the real deal, it is easy to find the fakes. Therefore, if you are going to detect Satan's lies, you must learn to recognize God's voice by being a lover of His Word. Then you will be able to easily spot Satan's lies and half-truths, and combat his accusations and his brutal voice of condemnation.

Never Yield Ground

One sin, even if it appears small and insignificant, can give the devil a foothold. "Go ahead, do it. You can get away with it. No one is watching." That might be true, but who's saying this to you? He's known as the "father of lies" for a reason. He's always looking for an opportunity to gain an advantage in your life.

While playing hide-and-seek, have you ever locked yourself behind a closed door? After time passes you think, *It's pretty quiet out there. I wonder where my brother is?* You decide to open the door just enough to peek outside only to find your older brother was right there all along. He quickly slides his foot between the door and the frame. From then on, he has the advantage, doesn't he? You are in a weak defensive position!

That is a picture of what it is like when curiosity gets us to open the door of our heart to sin. It gives Satan a foothold, and he pushes, continually applying pressure. If you don't call out to God for forgiveness and help, the sin will gain an advantage in your life. As in sports, the best defense is a strong offense. Do right, fear nothing! Run from sin, even the small ones. Don't let curiosity lead you to make stupid choices. Live in a way that pleases God. That will do for you what an old, fun song suggested, "Shut the door, keep the devil in the night. . . . Light the candle, everything is alright."* In other words, "Do not give the devil a foothold" (Ephesians 4:27). Keep the door of your heart closed to the devil and open only to the things of God.

Advance Courageously

In the heat of battle, seasoned soldiers tell us they never feel courageous. In fact, they describe feeling vulnerable, weak, and often confused by the chaos of war. So they have to trust in their training, fighting the way they learned. James 4:7 spells out the two-step battle plan every time we go into a fight:

Step 1: Submit yourself to God.
Step 2: Resist the devil.

Submitting your will to God when you are tempted to sin is not easy. But do it! Fight! Just pray, "Jesus, I am being tempted to (name it—be specific),

> "Submit yourselves, then, to God. Resist the devil, and he will flee from you. Come near to God and he will come near to you. Wash your hands, you sinners, and purify your hearts, you double-minded." —James 4:7–8

---

* "Shut De Do," Randy Stonehill, *Our Recollections*, Nashville: Word Records, 1996.

and I know that you would prefer that I (describe it—again, be specific). With your help, I choose to submit myself to Your will and to Your plans. I am Yours so I will do what You want. Satan, I resist your temptations, and I command you to leave me alone right now! In the powerful name of Jesus I pray, Amen."

The result is that the devil will take off packing, but don't be surprised if he quickly regroups and mounts a counterattack. Just keep doing the same two steps—submit to God and resist the devil—over and over. Train yourself. Each time you defeat him, you will get stronger, growing your courage and confidence in the Lord.

In summary, here's your operational plan: Stand with God; going it alone will lead to sure defeat. Be alert, you have an enemy who has drawn a bull's-eye on your back. Know Satan's tactics and God's truth. Never yield ground. Instead, advance courageously. God is with you and He is for you! Next, we look at battle gear you will need to win.

In Your Own Words:

1. If you charted your spiritual life on a continuum of 1 to 10 (1 means "I'm living my life independent of God," and 10 means the ideal, "I'm living my life dependent upon God"), where would you place yourself? Do you want to improve? If so, how will you do that?

2. What Scriptures will help you counter Satan's lies and tactics? Many are embedded in this chapter. What other biblical truths do you know?

3. Are there areas in your life you have compromised? Have you gone to God to help you shut Satan out? Have you gotten help from godly mentors?

In My Experience:

I was a preteen. My parents were under a lot of pressure that night. It was already late and we were to catch an early flight the next morning from La Paz to Cochabamba, Bolivia. My dad needed me to help with those little jobs I could easily perform so he could finish the things only he could do. If I didn't help, he might not get to sleep that night at all. But my attitude was wrong. I wanted to sleep instead.

In Bolivia we could only buy legal-sized paper that is three inches longer than the regular 8½ x 11" paper. He needed me to cut the extra off so it would work in our printer. Our large paper cutter was old and did a poor job if you did more than five sheets at a time. A feeling of despair rolled over me when I learned I'd have to prepare the entire ream. "Five hundred sheets of paper, five at a time. I'm doomed!"

I counted out the five sheets of paper just loud enough that my dad could hear my attitude. Once I placed them in the cutter I dropped the arm loudly. He ignored me. So I got quiet and started counting out seven or eight sheets, then ten or twelve. Instead of clean smooth cuts, the edges were jagged and slightly longer on one end. My dad could tell from the sound of the blade I was cutting too many sheets at a time. He warned me what would happen if I cut too many together. I acknowledged what he said, but ignored his instructions.

It's not easy to submit when you are of a mind to do something else. I justified my disobedience: "I want to sleep. The fact is, I'm a growing boy; I need to sleep!" My attitude grew more and more sour by the minute. In James 4:7–8 where we are told to submit to God and resist the devil, we are being asked to submit our will to God's wishes. That night I refused to submit my will to my dad's instructions.

I finished and placed the newly cut paper where it belonged. My dad loaded the printer and just as he had warned, the poorly cut paper printed crooked and jammed up. I had ruined an entire ream of paper. Though I had gotten the job done quickly, my poor workmanship revealed a serious characters flaw—an unwillingness to submit to my dad.

It was one thing to hear my dad's instructions; it was quite another to follow them. When God instructs us to submit to Him and resist the devil, He's instructing you to actually do what He asks. That's real submission. Unless you bring your will under His, you will lack God's spiritual protection. If you pray, "I submit," but continue to assert your own will, the devil will beat you until you fall and keep kicking you when you're down. Your enemy will show you no mercy.

When you accept Jesus, you are choosing Him to be your closest Friend and the undisputed Leader of your life. You are joining His kingdom, and coming under His authority, to do whatever He asks. As a Christ-follower, He promises you friendship, protection, and strength. But if you also try toying around with worldly things, you are showing contempt. James 4:4 tells us, "friendship with the world means enmity against God? Therefore, anyone who chooses to be a friend of the world becomes an enemy of God."

We show our love and devotion to God by doing what He asks: "If you love me, keep my commands" (John 14:15). Submitting to God's wishes is the ultimate battle.

If you are experiencing that struggle between doing what God wants and asserting yourself, you are not alone. I'm with you. We men are like wild stallions. Until we are bridled, we run aimlessly. But as we come under God's covering we live real and full lives.

Without allowing the Holy Spirit to bring you fully under God's leadership and authority, you remove yourself from His friendship, protection, and strength. Removing yourself from His covering makes you incapable of resisting the devil's attacks. Like that paper I cut, your life will at best print wrong, but more likely get jammed up.

That night I repaid my dad for the ream of paper I ruined. And I learned a lesson: obedience costs less than sin. You gain power in your life to the degree of your submission and no more. Any journey to manhood without daily submission to God will miss the mark. Submission to God empowers you to win.

Full Armor of God

"God is strong, and he wants you strong. So take everything the Master has set out for you, well-made weapons of the best materials. And put them to use so you will be able to stand up to everything the Devil throws your way. This is no afternoon athletic contest that we'll walk away from and forget about in a couple of hours. This is for keeps, a life-or-death fight to the finish against the Devil and all his angels.

"Be prepared. You're up against far more than you can handle on your own. Take all the help you can get, every weapon God has issued, so that when it's all over but the shouting you'll still be on your feet. Truth, righteousness, peace, faith, and salvation are more than words. Learn how to apply them. You'll need them throughout your life. God's Word is an indispensable weapon. In the same way, prayer is essential in this ongoing warfare. Pray hard and long. Pray for your brothers and sisters. Keep your eyes open. Keep each other's spirits up so that no one falls behind or drops out."

—Ephesians 6:10–18 (THE MESSAGE)

CHAPTER 10

Battle Gear

In Ephesians 6, Paul lists a number of very important qualities that make you strong for battle. He describes these as protective gear and weapons like those our modern soldiers wear. We must gear up with these qualities.

Helmet

Salvation is your helmet. The helmet reminds you who you are and protects your mind from attack. Like war, life can be confusing and frightening. Your parents may go through a rough patch in their relationship. A friend might turn on you. Sickness can strike you or someone you love. Salvation means knowing that you're God's beloved son, that you are never alone, and that He will guide you through the fog. The helmet also reminds you of your identity in Christ—a man of adventure with God, a man of Spirit-empowered character, a man of commitment to His task. This knowledge inspires you. Salvation protects your thinking.

Bulletproof Vest

Righteousness is your bulletproof vest. Do right, fear nothing! Living life the way God intends gives a confidence and strength nothing else can give. It protects your heart from divided loyalties—you love God and hate sin and its destructive nature. A divided heart loves God but enjoys sin, too. That kind of man is divided and unstable; he loses more battles than he wins and eventually gets taken out unless he repents. Righteousness protects your heart.

Utility Belt

Truth is your belt. Only God's Word, voice, and guidance can protect you and prepare you for victory. You must speak the truth,

think the truth, and live the truth. A lie will never protect you from defeat or prepare you for victory. In the same way that a belt is the place to carry the gear you most readily need, truth provides the basis for everything you do in the battle of life. Your choices, actions, and attitudes should always be grounded in the truth of God's Word. The truth protects you from shame, embarrassment, and defeat.

Combat Boots

Peace is your boots. The purpose of human warfare is to destroy and break things until the enemy can't fight anymore. Then, the winner stands on the rubble as though he were standing atop his own trophy and shouts victory!

You have to understand that the purpose of your fighting is very different. The kind of spiritual warfare godly men take part in does not bring destruction. Godly battle brings peace and freedom to people. Jesus came to reverse the damage of sin in people's lives, to set them free, and to give them peace and full lives. The boots you wear are not intended to transport you to places to deliver destruction but peace.

God wants those around you to be better off because you fought to bring God's peace into their chaotic lives.

God wants those around you to be better off because you fought to bring God's peace into their chaotic lives. And it will be just that, a battle for peace. Wherever Satan brings destruction, we fight alongside God to reverse what Satan has broken. Peace is the purpose of your fighting; peace protects you from fighting for selfish gain or misguided ends.

Riot Shield

Faith is your shield. Faith is knowing that the One you can't see will always come through for you; fear is thinking that what you can't see will harm you. Fear stirs up worry and resignation, and that makes you withdraw from the battle. In the midst of war, fear is common. You especially feel doomed when you are outnumbered and have no backup. Not so when you fight alongside God! He is always present in all His power to bring you through if you are prepared to fight His way. There is nothing Satan can throw at you or weapon he can use against you that you can't defeat with God's help. Faith in God protects you from fearing Satan and his evil plans by filling you with full confidence in God's presence and help.

Faith is knowing that the One you can't see will always come through for you; fear is thinking that what you can't see will harm you.

Assault Weapon

God's Word is your weapon of choice. As we have already learned, Satan is the father of lies. He attacks with lies and half-truths in the form of accusations and condemnation. God is truth. We can detect Satan's lies when we know God's Word.

You can fight back, win, and keep the upper hand by:

- Quoting Scriptures you have learned whenever you are tempted (Psalm 119:11).

- Standing firmly on God's truth as an unmovable foundation on which to build your life (Psalm 119:24).

- Using it as a flashlight to light your life's path (Psalm 119:105).

- Using it as a GPS system that provides turn-by-turn directions for life (Psalm 119:1).

- Using it as a polygraph machine to see past the lies of the enemy and see the truth of every situation (Psalm 119:29).

You must learn to use it well in the same way you would any other weapon. It takes daily training that involves reading the Word, thinking about what you learn, sharing it with others, asking questions of people who know God's Word well when you run across things you don't understand, and asking God to help you apply it to your life.

If you don't train to handle a gun, knife, or bow and arrow, you won't be able to use them well. So it is with God's Word. It is a powerful weapon that will bring victory to your life when you train and learn to use it well. God's Word protects you from Satan's lies and schemes.

Battlefield Communication

Prayer is your communication device. Soldiers would never think of going into battle without being wired into the command and control communications system. They know their commanding officers can see the big picture and can direct and advise them even in the toughest conditions.

It is the same with prayer. We talk with God, and He talks with us. Yes, God will talk with you. Read all the stories of the Bible, and you will see it is normal to converse with God and hear His voice. You read that right—hearing from God is normal! Develop the habit of talking with Him all day in every circumstance. Combine that with being a lover of God's Word, and you will soon develop the ability to hear His voice. There's nothing like it!

God's voice is unique and unmistakable:

- He will always encourage you and never tear you down.

- He will give you good advice and direction and never mislead you.

- He will correct you gently by convincing you to do right, not by condemning you.

- He will call you to be better and wiser, not make you feel small and stupid.

Prayer will protect you from going into battle blind and unaware of God's strategy for victory.

"Confess your sins to each other and pray for each other so that you may be healed." —James 5:16

Band of Brothers

Encouragement is how you build up your band of brothers. Never go into battle alone. Of course, God will go with you, but He intends for you to battle with a band of brothers next to you, side-by-side. Having men like your dad, godly mentors, and pastors is important. They have been your age and know the battles you are facing. They can help. Your Christian friends can also help. Encourage and pray for each other. Find a few guys you can share your needs with, knowing they will hold you accountable, pray with you, and help you. Do the same for them.

You are easy prey if you are alone. Satan's frequent lie is that if others know the battles you are facing they will think less of you. What he doesn't tell you is that the battles you face are the exact ones they face. Now that you know that, you can help each other without being judgmental. Encouragement protects you from losing courage and giving up.

Gear up from head-to-toe to do battle. You need:

- The helmet of *salvation*

- The bulletproof vest of *righteousness*

- The utility belt of *truth*

- Combat boots of *peace*

- The riot shield of *faith*

- Your assault weapon, *God's Word*

- Battlefield communication of *prayer*

- The mutual encouragement of a band of brothers

In Your Own Words:

1. Review each piece of battle gear described. List them and explain how can you move each from words on a page to actions in your life.

2. Read Ephesians 6:10–18 in five different Bible translations or paraphrases. Memorize the names of all eight pieces of gear; let the truth of this passage soak deep into your mind.

In My Experience:

In college, I wrote "The Armor Prayer" in my devotions, and I've used it through the years. It prepares me to fight battles God's way. Each statement relates to a piece of battle gear. Below each I've added comments describing how it has influenced my behavior.

- Remind me today who I am in You so I don't settle for anything less than Your best.

As a young man I carried the label "missionary kid." Don't get me wrong; I wore it proudly. But when your dad is the missionary, pastor, and Bible school director, everyone expects you to be an angel. After a while, I had to ask myself a tough question, "Am I behaving because people expect it or because I love God and want to become all He has designed?" At the root of the question was where my identity would come from. Was I just being a missionary kid or was I being God's son? I made a clear decision to be the latter. Have you settled this question in your own life?

- Make me righteous like You today so I can live right and fear nothing.

Another thing about being raised in a minister's home was a constant concern for how people viewed you. You don't dare wear clothes that are too nice or you'll be criticized; too homely and people will think you are a poor reflection on the church. Say too much or too little, and you might hurt someone's feelings. How do you say what is just right every time? The end result was a constant concern for people's opinions. The Bible suggests you can't easily please God if you fear what people think. Of course, I also feared what my classmates thought of me. The cure for insecurities and fears is holiness. Pleasing God gives you personal confidence and frees you from the fear of man. I concluded that if God is smiling I don't have to worry about how people see me. That set me free! Are you living to please God or man?

- Teach me Truth today so I don't fall for lies.

A guy one year ahead of me in high school built his life on a lie— that money could get him out of anything. His dad had lots of it.

The Armor Prayer

Remind me today who *I am in
You* so I don't settle for anything
less than Your best.

Make me *righteous* like
You today so I can live right
and fear nothing.

Teach me *Truth* today so
I don't fall for lies.

Help me today to defeat
destruction in someone's life
so they can enjoy Your *peace*.

Grow my *faith* today so I see
what You're up to in every
situation.

Give me a *Word* today so
I become strong in You.

Let's *talk* today so I feel
Your presence and receive
Your direction.

Keep me in *relationship*
with godly friends today so we
can encourage and challenge
one another.

—Doug Marsh

When this guy killed someone in a careless auto accident, his dad's money got him off the hook, but has yet to wipe away the guilt and shame and the health problems that resulted. When you build your life on truth, it is strong; when you build it on a lie, you are weak and will fail. The more you know God's ways, the more sure-footed you'll be throughout life. Are you building your life on the truth or a lie?

- Help me today to defeat destruction in someone's life so they can enjoy Your peace.

There were a few unpopular girls in my class. Some guys felt free to put them down. Sadly there were times I piled on. But that immediately stopped when I saw the pain our words inflicted. I asked God to forgive me, and I apologized to the girls. I wanted to be an agent of God's kindness. Where Satan had brought destruction, I wanted to deliver God's repair. What do your words and actions deliver compared to what they should?

- Grow my faith today so I see what You're up to in every situation.

It's always been easy for me to become frustrated when things don't turn out the way I had hoped or planned. But it takes a strong man of faith to look past the disappointment and see the new opportunity. I didn't date much in high school, but I did have two girls I really liked. Though I pursued, nothing developed with either. I was disappointed; I even doubted myself. "Don't I have what it takes to attract a girl?" But God was preparing a better relationship with someone else more suited for me. I met her as a sophomore in college and we married two years later. God is always looking out for your good even in the midst of difficult circumstances. We just need to ask Him, "Okay, God. What are You up to now? Where's the good You have planned?" It takes faith to ask Him and to look for it, and to patiently wait for His perfect plan to be fulfilled. Do you trust that God has your best interests in mind even when things seem out of control?

- Give me a Word today so I become strong in You.

I'm physically hungry every day. I need food to stay strong. I know the same is true of God's Word. But it is so easy for me to go days or weeks without jumping into the Bible. It can feel like such a chore. Guilt floods over me when I see my dusty Bible on the nightstand. Have you ever felt this way?

But one day I realized something. God didn't prepare His Word to condemn me. He gave it so I could joyfully experience Him. See how the truth can free you from a lie?

Today, I read the Word to be refreshed, not to check something off my daily to-do list. Sure, I need the discipline of consistency, but I don't beat myself up either. I read looking for God's invitation to adventure with Him—to actually do what He asks me to do. Throughout the day I repeat a verse to myself or remind myself of today's adventure. That makes it fun and refreshing. The result in hindsight is that God has given me strength others denied themselves because they didn't chose to be people of the Word. Is Bible reading still a chore for you or have you moved into the joy of adventuring with God? Ask God to help you, and He will.

> "Rejoice in the Lord always. I will say it again: Rejoice! Let your gentleness be evident to all. The Lord is near. Do not be anxious about anything, but in every situation, by prayer and petition, with thanksgiving, present your requests to God. And the peace of God, which transcends all understanding, will guard your hearts and your minds in Christ Jesus."
> —Philippians 4:4–7

- Let's talk today so I feel Your presence and receive Your direction.

I like to pray. Now I do, that is. Praying really took off for me when I learned to talk with God all day. When I face a decision I just ask, "God, what do you want me to do here? As I see it, there are two options. Are there others? If not, which is best?" He lets me know, too. When confronted by temptation I pray. When I receive good news, I say thank you. We just talk all day.

This conversational closeness makes my regular prayer time natural. I don't have to work myself up; I just close myself in with God and I pray about my thoughts and feelings and turn my worries and dreams into petitions. I especially like to pray over what I'm reading in the Word. As I think about people—those I love as well as those who irritate me—I pray for them. Everything I do, wherever I am, I talk with God. Have you ever realized prayer could be a constant ongoing conversation with God all day? Try it!

- Keep me in relationship with godly friends today so we can encourage and challenge one another.

This doesn't often come natural to us guys. You know, making a conscious effort to have peers and godly men in your life that will keep you accountable spiritually. To be strong men we need a band of brothers. This doesn't come natural to me. I'm private and independent. But I've learned nothing makes me stronger than relating well with other godly men.

In high school, I had such a friend in David Thomas. We were friends, but we also added a greater purpose to our friendship by holding each other accountable. We talked to each other about our spiritual fitness, looked for counsel from God's Word, and prayed together. We were competitors in track, weekend mountaineers together on the Inca Trails in Bolivia, and incurable adventure seekers. I also had godly men who invested in my life—David North, Doug Ayres, Herman Lima, Marceal Apaza, George Davis, Eugene Hunt, Gary Miller, and others who are just names to you but heroes to me. Each shared strength with me in unique ways.

As young men, we find it hard to admit we don't know what we don't know. We feel that being in a learning posture before others might minimize us. But nothing can be further from the truth. God wants to use you to make those around you stronger, and He wants others to strengthen you. I like the idea of others benefiting from my strength, but I must humble myself to let the strength of others build me. Becoming a real man can only take place in the company of godly men.

Guys wonder why they struggle with the same things year after year in their life. It's largely because they are living isolated lives, separating themselves from one of God's sources of victory—other godly peers and men. Who are the peers you lean on and the godly men you look up to for help? Who are you intentionally offering strength to?

> "WE HAVE AN OBLIGATION—
> BUT IT IS NOT TO THE FLESH,
> TO LIVE ACCORDING TO IT."
>
> **Romans 8:12**

CHAPTER 11

You Have
What It Takes

Our enemy is the father of lies, and one of his worst lies is that young men cannot be pure. He convinces the world that holiness is impossible, and that it's not worth making the effort because young men aren't capable of controlling themselves. The lie suggests you are broken and hopeless and that any effort to be a godly man is pointless. Not so! The objective of the lie is to make you give up, to grow accustomed to sinning, and to accept life at a low level.

Paul debunks this lie. You "have an obligation—but it is not to the flesh [sinful nature], to live according to it" (Romans 8:12). You aren't doomed! Don't assume defeat. God is with you, and God is for you. You can be the man God wants you to be.

In Romans 8, Paul goes on to further refute this lie:

- You are not a slave to fear. All this talk about being a warrior, having a battle to fight, and an enemy who is out to get you might sound scary and overwhelming, but you have

"Therefore, brothers and sisters, *we have an obligation— but it is not to the flesh, to live according to it.* For if you live according to the flesh, you will die; but if by the Spirit you put to death the misdeeds of the body, you will live. For those who are led by the Spirit of God are the children of God. *The Spirit you received does not make you slaves, so that you live in fear again; rather, the Spirit you received brought about your adoption to sonship.* And by him we cry, 'Abba, Father.' The Spirit himself testifies with our spirit that we are God's children."

—Romans 8:12–16 (emphasis added)

a loving Heavenly Father who is on your side. That should chase fear away and fill you with confident strength. God is with you. He's teaching you how to fight and overcome, letting you in on His winning strategies. Don't be afraid! You can be a godly man.

- You are not orphaned. An orphan boy is left on his own. He feels abandoned, left to defend himself without anyone bigger and stronger to stand next to him. He believes that if anything good is to happen it will be his to achieve alone. But that is not so! Ask any orphan who has been chosen and adopted by a great family; the feelings of abandonment are gone. When you give your life over to Jesus, He adopts you into His family and fathers you. God is always next to you, guiding you, coaching you, advising you, and empowering you. You are not abandoned and you are not alone. The eternal and infinite, all-powerful, all-knowing, everywhere-present God is with you.

- You are God's son! God takes His sons into His confidence, helps them, and protects them. You are prized by God. In Him you are safe and strengthened. He gives His sons everything they need to win.

Anytime you feel fear or abandonment—when you sense you are inadequate, not up to the challenge set before you—you will be tempted to be passive or to be abusive. Neither is the right response for a son of God. Before we talk about the right way to square your shoulders and confront the challenges you are facing, let's look at what it means to be passive and what it means to be abusive.

Adam: A Passive Man

In the Garden of Eden, Adam chose to be passive. He did not fight for Eve to make the right choice. He stood next to her and silently watched her disobey God. Then, he ate the forbidden fruit himself. By choosing to be passive, Adam chose Eve over God. Being passive, that is having an unwillingness to stand in your God-given strength and fight, equals denying God. Adam's passivity introduced sin to the human race, and that impacts you even today.

But we convince ourselves it is all right to be passive because it will be safe, which is code for taking the path of least resistance, and it will keep us from rocking the boat too much, which is code for being afraid to stand for what is right. Passivity is not a manly quality! It is Satan's way of making you cower and yield to feelings of fear and abandonment that will drive you away from God.

Samson: An Abusive Man

Samson, the Old Testament judge, sometimes acted abusively. God had given him supernatural strength to serve others and protect them, but at times he chose to be abusive. He burned fields, vandalized property, and did other things to hurt others and show off. God has given you strength too, but unlike Samson, you need to choose to use it to help others and not to harm them.

Men who respond to challenges by acting abusively toward people usually feel like they are being forced to do things they don't want to do. They may feel inadequate, small, and like they are not in control of things. Unlike the passive response, which is to fade into the background, the abuser acts up.

Abusers attempt to protect their small or fragile ego by an over-the-top display of physical strength like pushing or hitting, verbal abuse such as swearing or putting people down, or emotional manipulation like stomping off or behaving in a quiet, angry manner.

Abuse is selfish behavior intended to protect oneself by an inappropriate demonstration of power. But God gave you manly strength to stand up and protect others. When Samson died, his life assignment, to deliver Israel from the clutches of the Philistines, remained incomplete. His effort to protect his own ego left his people enslaved.

Jesus: A Perfect Man

Adam acted passively. Samson acted abusively. The feelings down inside were the same. They both felt fear and abandonment, and their responses were opposite but equally damaging. Neither felt they were up to the challenge before them. They responded poorly and the consequences were devastating.

Jesus showed us the right response. He was neither passive nor abusive. To be passive is to live as a spectator. To be abusive is to assume it all depends on you alone. It's an angry, emotional, and often thoughtless and impulsive reaction that says, "I must set things straight here and now myself." Jesus was engaged and fully present, never the sissy who watched life pass by. He was assertive, too, while depending entirely on His Father to help Him know exactly when and how to respond to injustice. Jesus took His feelings to His Father in prayer.

In the Garden of Gethsemane, Jesus expressed His feelings to His Father: "Let this cup pass." But He knew to stand up and quietly and resolutely go to the cross. He was not passive, because no one took Jesus' life; He gave it freely. Nor was He abusive. He had feelings and fear, which He expressed to the Father, but He didn't sidestep His responsibilities. That is the way to respond when we feel alone or fearful.

The result of Adam's passive behavior was sin. The result of Samson's abusiveness was slavery. Jesus' mature, manly response brought life for all who believe in Him.

God wants to sharpen and strengthen you to grow into the man He intends for you to become. The promise is that those who call on God as their Father will "put to death the misdeeds of the body" (Romans 8:13) and truly live. So walk in the confidence that God is your Father.

Whenever feelings of fear or inadequacies overwhelm you, call on your Heavenly Father, "Father, I'm feeling overwhelmed and am tempted to shrink back or act up. Help me confront this challenge with the confidence and wisdom that is promised to me as Your son." God will lead people into your life to help you in those moments. They will be God's hands extended. He will give you creative responses and timely advice and direction. You are not alone because you are God's son. In Christ, you have what it takes to be a godly man.

In Your Own Words:

1. Read and reflect on Romans 8:12–16. What exactly is it saying? How can you live its message?

2. When do you feel afraid or have feelings of being alone in the world? Do you take those feelings to God? To godly men in your life? Why or why not?

3. Think back on times when you might have acted passively, abusively, or with the right response in the face of battles, disappointments, or setbacks. What can you learn from those experiences to become a better man?

In My Experience:

My story is one of confidence and support. I'm from a strong Christian family. I learned early to confide in God, to trust the support of my family, and to be grateful to our church for the opportunities their love provided. The very fact that I got to grow up overseas, to be bilingual, to participate in helping people in Peru and Bolivia know Jesus was because faithful people in our U.S. churches were willing to support my family financially. I grew up in an extremely supportive environment.

But that may not be your story. Perhaps your parents are divorced or you don't enjoy the support of a godly family. That was my dad's story. His father lived a wicked life and eventually divorced his mom. When my dad was six, his neighbor led him to the Lord. As soon as his dad, my grandfather, learned about it, he did what he could to undermine my dad's faith in God.

Another family member tried to lure my dad to drink beer as early as eight years of age. But my dad never partook, thanks to the quiet resolve of his godly mother. In his teens, my dad felt directed to ministry but his father objected. He offered to pay for my dad's college tuition if he agreed to study in a state university to become a mining engineer, but vowed my dad would receive nothing if he attended Bible college. My dad obeyed his Heavenly Father instead. My dad had every reason to be fearful and to feel abandoned. But God provided for all his needs.

My dad broke a downward spiral in our family line. His dad was an alcoholic. If he had drunk the beer offered him as a child, he too could have become a drunk. Instead my dad followed Christ. He provided his family the strong home life he was denied. He practiced sacrificial love for my mother that his own dad never modeled. Where did he learn to do that? From God, His Word, and godly counsel.

Maybe your life isn't picture perfect. But since you're reading this book, you likely have a mentor in your life that belongs to a Bible-believing church. Its members stand ready to help you the same way the Assembly of God church in Lone Pine, California, helped my dad when he was just a boy. Though my grandfather abandoned my dad and his mom, the church supported them. God did what He promised, to be "a father to the fatherless" (Psalm 68:5).

You have everything you need to step into the bright future God has planned for you. You are not a victim of circumstance. You are not a slave to fear. You are not abandoned. Your life right now may not be ideal, but you are not doomed. Your story today isn't the final chapter. Entrust your tomorrow to God by living for Him every day. As you do, God will come through for you. My dad did it, and I'm glad he did!

Strength for Uncompromising Men

You want to be a strong young man. You want the ability to square your shoulders when the enemy of your soul attacks and win. God offers you His strength as you learn to trust Him and fight. There are many battles young men commonly face. As you grow in your adventures with God, you will learn to rely on Him, and He will lead you to victory. As His son, you don't have to assume failure or settle for a compromised life. You can face battles and win!

There is a confident strength that belongs only to those who live life God's way—to those who adventure with God, do battle His way, and live out their God-given task. It is a confidence reserved for those who know that God is pleased with them, and it leads to an inner strength that shows up in every area of life. They are the qualities we see in men of uncompromising character that we admire.

Uncompromising men of God know their source of in these areas.

Protection

Your greatest protection is your integrity. Integrity means wholeness. You do not have a divided heart. You are not one person at church and another at school and another at home. You walk with God every day and do what pleases Him. You are a young man of character everywhere, whether alone or in the presence of others. The temptation for many young men is to lie. You make a mistake or cut a corner and get found out. Do you lie and cover it up, or do you tell the truth?

A lie promises to give you something it can't deliver—protection. The lie goes like this, "If I lie, I shield myself from embarrassment or punishment." The lie deceives you because often you actually do get away with it for a while, maybe even a long time. Then, you begin to live a lie, faking your way through life. The lie promised protection but led to fear of being found out. You don't feel safe around people because you are afraid you will be exposed.

The battle uncompromising men win is the battle for godly integrity. It is their source of safety. That is something a lie can never deliver.

Manhood

Every guy wants to prove he has what it takes to be a real man. That desire is incredibly strong because God himself put it there. Only God can truly fill this need. The problem comes when you look for this stamp of approval from someone or something other than God. The answer that comes back from false sources can make you feel very good for a while, but ultimately will leave you empty, ashamed, and confused.

One of the wrong places guys often find themselves seeking this approval is from girls. God made girls to reflect His beauty and mercy, so naturally we should and do find them highly attractive. That is by God's design. However, God did not create femininity to settle your deep question, "Am I a real man?" Only God can answer that.

Many young men today do what Adam did in the Garden. When faced with the choice between God and the girl, they often choose the beautiful girl they can see over God whom they cannot see. A guy might push the limits with a young lady and brag about it in the locker room as though his actions prove he is a man. Wrong! She is not a conquest to be taken; she is a priceless princess, a child of God.

You are made to offer her strength, to give her protection, and to love her at a high cost to yourself. That price is battling back the urges to lust after her and act inappropriately toward her, taking what she should rightly give only to her husband on the night of their marriage. When you take from a girl what is not yours to be had, even if she offers it, you act weak in your lust. God did not create you to take from her but rather to give her protection. You may need to help protect her from her own choices. Doing so will protect you as well.

How do you find the source of true manhood? The answer is found in God. Let Him initiate you into manhood. He will give you the answer as you grow in His Word. Make it a daily habit. Don't just read it; that's boring. Live it! Look for every time God calls you on adventure. Those calls are easy to find if you're alert. If He says, "Be truthful," and you realize you have lied, you immediately ask forgiveness and for His help to be honest. That is a call to adventure, a call to depend on Him. No more hiding behind deceit. You are called to square your shoulders and be truthful, to be a man of integrity.

As you pay special attention to obey these calls to adventure, you will discover God is helping you. Over time you will develop a confidence that only comes by taking your question to God and accepting His invitations to adventure. God will not speak a quick and empty, "Oh, yes, of course, you have what it takes!" What He will do is guide you on adventures so you discover that in Him you really do have what it takes.

In addition to His Word, God will use other godly boys and men to teach you and to challenge you. Look for guys who are also adventuring with God, accepting His every call to obey Him. Together you can discover the answer to this deep and important question. Don't seek it alone; go with God and with godly men by your side.

This critically important question, "Do I have what it takes to be a man?" can never be answered by a girl. Instead, take it to God and to godly men who are committed to living out the adventures presented in the Word. An important side benefit to relying on God to answer this question can be summed up in a wise saying fathers once passed onto their sons, "An ounce of confidence is worth more than a pound of good looks." When you discover you are a real man because of your growing trust in the Lord, that confidence will attract quality girls and protect you from worldly ones. Noble girls are attracted to guys with godly confidence and will stick with them.

The safety you offer her from your deep godly strength will serve as a foundation that will benefit you and your future. She will be so grateful to have found a true man who goes to God for His strength because she can depend on you to offer that strength to her. The security and happiness that will provide her and the trust she will have in you will far exceed any short-term "conquests" you might enjoy today. Live for God's stamp of approval on your life every day!

Provision

God takes care of men by giving them talents and abilities to be creative, to make money, to provide for their families, and to be generous. God is proud of young men who learn a strong work ethic.

Unfortunately, our culture encourages boys to value entertainment over hard work. There is nothing wrong with having fun, but it should be balanced with effort, accomplishment, and a love for hard work. Without this balance, you run the risk of becoming lazy and getting into trouble.

King Solomon said, "All hard work brings a profit, but mere talk leads only to poverty" (Proverbs 14:23) and "One who is slack in his work is brother to one who destroys" (Proverbs 18:9).

The most extreme form of laziness is theft, taking what others have worked for. Paul wrote, "Anyone who has been stealing must steal no longer, but must work, doing something useful with their own hands, that they may have something to share with those in need" (Ephesians 4:28).

The opposite of laziness is being a workaholic. These are guys who work too much. They don't take enough time to play and hang out with friends and family. King Solomon might have been a workaholic. He said, "So I hated life, because the work that is done under the sun was grievous to me" (Ecclesiastes 2:17). But he wouldn't suggest laziness either. He knew it was important to work, "A person can do nothing better than . . . find satisfaction in their own toil. This too, I see, is from the hand of God" (Ecclesiastes 2:24).

Both of these extremes—laziness and overworking—deny God the place He deserves as your Provider. They rob you of the inner assurance that He will take care of you. These extremes make you take things into your own hands and either cut corners or work yourself to the bone. Both extremes are wrong. The battle is to keep a good balance.

Reputation

You are who God says you are, and not the person that others claim you are. You are not defined by the stuff you own and how it makes you feel. You are God's son. That is where you draw your status, your value, and your identity. God will be your Father and make you the very best version of you possible. As He does, you draw your worth from Him. He offers true status and stature.

Many young men step into a trap, the pitfall of drawing their reputation or status from the friends they hang out with, the clothes they wear, and the things they buy. Of course, friends are important, and no one expects you to ignore today's styles and to dress like Moses from the Old Testament. But you should not allow friends, styles, and possessions to give you something to boast or be prideful about. Paul writes, "Let the one who boasts boast in the Lord" (2 Corinthians 10:17).

Humbly ask God to shape you into His character every day so that your thoughts, words, and actions make Him look good. In time, you will discover that He is a sure foundation on which to build your life. Your friends will have off days, styles will change, and things will break. Chasing these things to get status will leave you bankrupt! God will never have an off day; He will always be there for you and will never change or break. He is a rock! So draw strength from Him rather than these other things. Then, you will be able to share His strength with your friends. When styles change and things get lost, you might feel bad, but your world will not be shaken.

The battle is to draw your status, worth, and identity from God, not anyone or anything else. If Satan can get you fixated on what others think of whom you hang with, what you wear, and the cool stuff you flash around, he will make you weak and easy to take out. Building your life on what others think of you is unwise. Build your life on what God thinks of you instead. That is the battle!

Integrity

When Adam and Eve sinned, they were ashamed and hid themselves, hoping God would not notice. Perhaps they thought they could live a double life—with God seeing them one way while they lived another. But He did see their sin, and He will always see you for who and what you really are. It does no good to fake it. God, and eventually others, will always discover the real you.

Satan would like you to adopt a double life, preferring a false public image above the private reality. He would love for you to act like a spiritual person at church and around parents and others, but live a very different life with your school friends or when you're alone. Satan will be happy to let you act like you're spiritual at church and worldly at school. But you want to be the real deal no matter where you are or whom you're with. John, one of Jesus' disciples, wrote a letter from Jesus to a church that said, "You have a reputation of being alive, but you are dead" (Revelation 3:1). The public image was one thing, but the reality was another. You should refuse to live that way!

You are to battle for substance over image. You don't want to look like a strong man; you want to be a strong man! So don't live a split life. Be true and honest; do what's right when people are looking and when they are not, when people praise you and when they don't. Live every moment to hear the applause of God.

Religion

At school and throughout life, you will interact with people of other religions and belief systems, and probably with some people who choose not to believe in God at all. The Bible makes it very clear that salvation can only be found in a faith relationship with God through Jesus Christ. "Salvation is found in no one else, for there is no other name under heaven given to mankind by which we must be saved" (Acts 4:12). Everyone needs a Savior and only Jesus is that Savior. In Galatians, Paul warns about allowing anyone to throw you off course. Any gospel that does not point you to the divine Jesus is false (see Galatians 1:8).

You will need to stand firm in this relationship and be patient and kind toward those who haven't accepted Christ as their Savior. They will be watching you. If you are careful with them, especially when they make fun of you, they will be drawn to the truth of the gospel. You will have to be strong.

It might come as a surprise to you, but Satan doesn't mind religion at all. What he hates is relationship with God. He knows that people who enter into friendship with Jesus will become more and more what God designed them to be. That is the last thing Satan wants. Religious and even moral people don't bother him.

Religions can be appealing to people, and there are a couple of things that Satan really likes about them. Religions give people a false sense of security by letting them think, "If I go to church, the temple, the mosque, or the synagogue and follow the rules, I'll be okay." They also create a sense of independence by suggesting, "I don't have to bend my knee to Jesus Christ." We are not saved because we follow religious rules, rituals, and traditions but because we have a personal, growing relationship with Jesus Christ, making Him our best Friend and the Leader of our lives.

The battle here includes two things: First, never let your relationship with God turn into keeping rules, duty, and routine. Instead, keep your friendship with God alive and new every day. Stay in the Word, talk with God, and serve those around you. Second, don't be fooled by false religions. A false religion is any spiritual system that adds to, subtracts from, divides, or multiplies the Word of God. Any religion that does not point you to God through Jesus Christ alone is false. Don't be fooled.

Defense

God gives young men like you strength to stand up and defend yourself and others when attacked. That strength is not given for revenge. It is right to defend your reputation when falsely accused, but you must never cross into retaliation: "I'll show him! He'll be sorry he ever crossed me." Letting God avenge a wrong committed against you takes a deep level of trust and is hard to practice. God says, "It is mine to avenge; I will repay" (Deuteronomy 32:35). You naturally want to take matters into your own hands whenever you feel slighted or hurt, but you should develop a heart that cannot be offended and that refuses to harbor bitterness and anger. If your heart trusts God to defend you, He will protect you from one of Satan's greatest weapons—deadweight. Dragging offenses with you throughout life will keep you from going far with God and with others.

Allowing bitterness and anger to drive you to get even will hold you back in every area of your life. Let it go by forgiving people when they hurt you. Trust God to set people straight. He can and will do it! That requires real backbone and real trust. Doing so makes you free and alive, free of bitterness and anger.

God is your source of strength and confidence. Anyone or anything that takes God's place in your life will leave you empty. Battle any counterfeits that replace God as the center of your life. The Old Testament prophets called anything that became a substitute for God an idol. Idols say they'll deliver what God promises, but can never come through. Only God can come through for you and make you into the strong, confident man He designed you to become.

In Your Own Words:

1. Reflect on the challenges presented in this chapter one at a time and write a one-sentence commitment statement for each of them. To begin, open each with the words "I will…" These statements are important because uncompromising men make good pre-decisions.

2. What pressures are you feeling to compromise the things you know are right? Pray and invite Jesus into each. Write a commitment statement for these as well. Who can you talk to about these?

In My Experience:

It's much easier to win battles when you expect them because you can prepare. Governments spend millions of dollars gathering intelligence for this very reason. They don't want to be taken by surprise.

As a young boy and teen, I was very observant. Perhaps that is the advantage of being the youngest in the family. I learned a lot by watching my older brother and sister. If they got in trouble I made sure to avoid their mistakes. Likewise, when they did something right, I followed their example.

I also listened to Bible stories over and over. The men and woman of the Bible illustrate successes and failures. Moses, Daniel, Josiah, Johanadab, and Peter are among my favorites. Isn't it intriguing that God didn't hide their flaws? Biographies of great men inspired me, too, like Hudson Taylor, Brother Andrew, Jim Elliot, and Dietrich Bonhoeffer. Historical figures like George Washington, John Adams, Abraham Lincoln, American circuit riding preachers like Peter Cartwright, and men like John Wesley, William Wallace, and Martin Luther King, Jr. are all greats. And men I admired surrounded me as well. My dad was at the top of that list.

Not only was I inspired by their stories, I realized their circumstances were unique but their battles were the same I was facing in my own way. And their experiences prepared me for challenges I'd face later. Their lives helped me live up to the call of 1 Timothy 4:12: "Don't let anyone look down on you because you are young, but set an example for the believers in speech, in conduct, in love, in faith and in purity." What better way to set an example than to stand on the shoulders of men who had won and lost battles I can learn from? It's easier to win battles you can anticipate and prepare for, and it's best when you can avoid them altogether.

CHAPTER 13

The Great Empowerment

So what is your life's battle? What's your big quest? What dragons must you slay?

Is your battle to stand against sin? Is it to oppose the devil? Is it to endure temptations until you get to heaven? Is it to simply survive? It might come as a surprise, but the answers are no, no, no, and no.

Your battle is to become the man God designed you to be and to share His strength with others. Your quest is to be in love with God, to be full of His Holy Spirit's power for life, and to be on task. Why? That makes Jesus look good. You were created for one reason and one reason alone—to bring glory to God by making Him look good. The more your life brings glory to God the more you become the best version of you possible.

> Every right choice you make in public and private forges you into a man whose character reflects the character of Christ.

This is not a life of defense, or just holding on until Jesus comes. Oh no! You should live in an offensive posture, moving forward. The call is to be a real man who brings glory to God. You don't cower in fear or hunker down. Instead, stand up and live life to the max. Advance! Go on adventure with God and battle to become the man God designed you to be. As you do, you share your strength with others.

Every obstacle you encounter is a battle to become the man God designed you to be—a man of great adventure and faith, of strength and courage in battle, and of purpose and determination in life. When you face a challenge, the essential question is this, "Who's going to get the credit in this battle? God or Satan?" Your goal is to reflect Christ's character. Every right choice you make in public and private forges you into a man whose character reflects the character of Christ. That makes you an overcomer! And God offers His very own power for young men who want to be winners.

The Holy Spirit

The Holy Spirit is God's power source in your life, and you will need all of His strength to become the man that He designed you to be. When you accepted Jesus as your King and submitted yourself entirely to Him, His Spirit took up residence in your life. That is how close He is to you. His Spirit lives in you and gives you power and help in a number of important ways:

- *He befriends you.* Jesus, when He went back to heaven, promised to send the Holy Spirit to come alongside you and be your Friend. The Holy Spirit takes Jesus' place as God's tangible presence in your everyday life. He is your Advisor on decisions, someone you can talk to, and someone you can trust (John 14:16–18, 25–27).

- *He convicts you.* The Holy Spirit always tries to convince you to do what is right. Your goal is to listen carefully and obey fully. He will never beat you down but will try to lift you up and point you back to Christ (John 16:8–11).

- *He will lead you through the fog of battle to victory, if you listen.* The Holy Spirit speaks at the same volume—He seldom shouts, and He seldom whispers. If you consistently ignore His voice, you will find it harder and harder to hear Him. But as you do what He asks, you will develop an ear to hear His voice more clearly.

- *He guides you.* He helps you learn God's plans for your life and keeps you in God's will. You can know it is the Holy Spirit who is guiding you because He always leads you in a way that is consistent with God's Word (John 16:13).

About the Holy Spirit, Jesus said, "He will glorify me" (John 16:14). The Holy Spirit makes Jesus look good in your life by giving you good advice, by encouraging you to make right choices, and by calling you to follow Him. When you obey the voice of the Holy Spirit, God will shape you into the man He designed you to be.

The Baptism in the Holy Spirit

God's Spirit is present in the life of everyone who has surrendered his will to the Father by asking Jesus to be his Friend and the Leader of his life. But there is an added gift of power that Jesus gives to those who are baptized in the Holy Spirit. It is not something you earn, but a gift you are instructed to ask for and seek. Jesus is the giver of the gift. The baptism in the Holy Spirit helps you become the man God designed you to be. He gives you His strength to win battles and to be God's ally in this world.

As a Christian, you have a responsibility to seek the baptism in the Holy Spirit. Jesus is eager to give you His gift of power. You will know you have received the baptism in the Holy Spirit when you pray and worship God in a language you have never studied or learned. It is the first outward sign that you have received this gift. There are examples of this in Acts chapters 2, 10, and 19. It's like a receipt that demonstrates that you have received His special power. It doesn't end there because that is just the first evidence. As you walk in that power, you will find you are becoming more alive in Christ, that you have more joy, that you are more eager to tell others about what God is doing in your life, and that you are more courageous and bold in the adventures you take with God.

There is no specific formula to receive the baptism in the Holy Spirit. Since Jesus is the Baptizer, your goal should be to seek Him regularly, to deepen your love for Him, and to ask Him to baptize you in the Holy Spirit. The key is seeking the Giver, Jesus, and asking Him for the gift. James 4:8 says, "Come near to God and he will come near to you."

Here's how to get closer to Jesus:

Wash it! Live with *a clean heart.* Follow God in everything you think, say, and do, and battle to become the man God designed you to be.	Repent and be baptized, every one of you, in the name of Jesus Christ for the forgiveness of your sins. And you will receive the gift of the Holy Spirit (Acts 2:38).
Want it! Live with *a heart of desire.* Go for everything God has for you and never settle for "just enough." Go for it all!	But if from there you seek the Lord your God, you will find him if you seek him with all your heart and with all your soul (Deuteronomy 4:29).
Word it! Live with *a heart of faith.* Believe and trust God's Word, take every call for obedience in the Bible as an invitation to adventure with God, and never turn Him down.	Therefore I tell you, whatever you ask for in prayer, believe that you have received it, and it will be yours (Mark 11:24).
Worship! Live with *a heart of praise and thanks.* Focus on how big God is, and He will shape His character into you.	Then they believed his promises and sang his praise (Psalm 106:12).

Work It! Live with *an obedient heart.* Know that strength will flow in your life as you do whatever He asks you.	We are witnesses of these things, and so is the Holy Spirit, whom God has given to those who obey him (Acts 5:32).

The power of the Holy Spirit will help you become the man of character God designed you to be!

In Your Own Words:

1. When has the Holy Spirit been your Friend, convicted you, and guided your life? How did His personal presence make you better?

2. Refer to Acts 2:4, 10:44–46, and 19:5–6 and describe the common experience people had when they received the baptism in the Holy Spirit.

3. Have you been baptized in the Holy Spirit? If you have, think about how you can more effectively use His power. If not, begin to seek His empowerment now.

In My Experience:

I received the baptism in the Holy Spirit at camp when I was eight or nine years old. I went to the altar and prayed for a while until I received. I was so excited! I felt like I could charge through a wall.

But I had been asking Jesus to baptize me for a couple of years. The truth is I had sought so long I became discouraged at one point. In fact, I thought *If it is this hard to get a gift, it must not be real.* My dad sensed my frustration and sympathized with the feelings I was experiencing. He gave me some very good advice. It was simply to seek the Giver of the gift, and not the gift itself.

He explained that God had plenty of power for my life, but that power comes from Him. His Holy Spirit wants to have relationship with me just like I want with my own family and friends. If I went after my friends for money or gifts without any interest in them, I'd probably get little or nothing. So it is with God. As we seek Him, He pours His power out.

This helped me a lot. I hope this advice helps you, too. That night at kids camp in Missouri, I just talked with Jesus. I reminded Him again how much I loved Him, and how I wanted to give Him my whole life. My heart started to overflow with praise for Him, and after a while my words turned to a language I had never learned before.

For weeks after that, I spent time in prayer in my dad's camper. I'd lie on the bed over the truck cab and just praise the Lord. And soon I'd start to flow in my new prayer language again. As a result, I started to develop a greater passion for Christ. And more than anything, it has drawn me into a deeper relationship with God and given me a greater concern for those who don't know Jesus. A new boldness and a great level of persistence have come to characterize my life. I can't imagine settling for a life that didn't include this amazing presence and power in my life. And I hope you don't either.

Grow Your Character

Here are three important adventures for every young believer to undertake in order to grow godly character.

Read Your Bible

The Bible is God's Word and you will gain strength by learning everything it teaches. Start by reading the New Testament Book of Mark. It is a fun, action-filled book telling the story of Jesus.

If you want some help understanding it better, I'd suggest you get a good study Bible. My preferred version for guys is the Fire Bible. There is an edition for elementary-aged boys, teen guys, and adults, too. It has great notes and articles that will make God's Word come alive. Make it your daily practice to read, pray, and memorize His Word. As you do, you will grow strong in faith and character, and will be equipped to resist temptation (Psalm 119:11).

Be Baptized in Water

Water baptism is a public confession of your belief in Jesus Christ and your commitment to follow Him your whole life. Jesus asks everyone who comes to faith in Him to be baptized in water as an act of obedience (Acts 2:38). Being baptized is not what saves you, but it honors Christ when we obey Him. If you have yet to be baptized, this is an important adventure God wants you to take. Talk with your pastor about obeying Jesus by being baptized in water as soon as you can.

Tithe

Tithing is the biblical principle of giving the first 10 percent of your earnings to the Lord. Malachi 3:10 states, "'Bring the whole tithe into the storehouse, that there may be food in my house. Test me in this,' says the LORD Almighty, 'and see if I will not throw open the floodgates of heaven and pour out so much blessing that you will not have room enough to store it.'" The storehouse is your local church. Bring the first 10 percent of your allowance or the money you make from side jobs, summer jobs, gifts, and other income and give it to the church for the advancement of the ministry. Everything you have belongs to God, and He asks that you return 10 percent to Him to show your gratitude, dependence, and devotion. He even promises to reward your obedience with more blessings than you can contain. What a great promise from God!

Battle-Tested Character: Jim Barger

The journey to becoming a man of God is unique for everyone. Many men spend their entire lives in church, never straying from the path God has laid out for them. This is the best choice. Some, however, drift from the way of God and follow their own path, making poor choices as they go. Thankfully, God is able to redeem the fallen man and set him on the true path. He is able to take a story of tragedy and make it a story of triumph. This is the story of Jim Barger.

Jim grew up in a Christian home, having been adopted as a toddler by a loving family. Never spoiled, Jim's family taught him the value of hard work and discipline, while also instilling values of faith and reliance on God.

Jim Barger

Jim recalls when he chose to accept Christ and follow His plan:

"During sixth grade, Ding Tuling, an artist, held a revival at my church. He would illustrate his message by drawing chalk pictures. When he arrived at the main point of the message, he would focus a black light on the easel to reveal a picture that was 'hidden' under the one we had seen him draw. That absolutely astonished me. I responded to an altar call and made Jesus my best Friend."

As a teenager, Jim's faith faltered as he became entrenched in worldly things. Jim's story isn't one of a single dramatic choice to reject God. What happened in Jim's life is what happens to most young people in his position. Little by little, the things of God became less important to him. Attending church, reading the Bible, and prayer were replaced with riding his motorcycle and spending time with people who were a bad influence on him.

Jim recognizes that his story is hardly unique, and he challenges other young people to learn from his mistakes. "Every man experiences tests as he journeys from boyhood to manhood. Many experiences are universal; every man will go through them at some point. How he handles the tests will forever shape his character."

Jim decided that instead of following his father's advice to attend college, he would enter the Marines. God protected Jim through this experience, and ultimately used it to make Jim who He wanted him to be. In the military, Jim learned electronics in a way that would help him establish a successful career after his tour of duty. Even when he rebelled against authority, God was able to use it for good.

When Jim reached the age of thirty, he rarely attended church with his wife. He mistakenly believed that since he walked away from his faith when he was younger, God could no longer save him. One Sunday, Jim reluctantly went to church with his family, and the text of the sermon changed his life. "Imagine my joy when I did go to church and the pastor preached on Psalm 51, explaining that David's sin of adultery had led to a man's death but God forgave him and loved him. The pastor gave an altar call, and I responded. In my haste to get to the front of the church, I nearly knocked down the pastor's son-in-law, who asked if I wanted him to come with me."

After Jim renewed his commitment to Christ, he was challenged in many ways. Jim felt strongly that God wanted to use him to minister to others, but he had no idea what that meant. He didn't know if he should quit his comfortable job and become a full-time pastor or if he should become a leader for young men in his church. God's voice told him to be patient and to walk through the doors that opened for him.

After a few years of leading young men to Christ and mentoring them in the faith in a boy's program called Royal Rangers, the Spirit prompted Jim to leave his well-paying job and become an independent consultant and contractor. This was a huge risk financially, but because the Spirit was guiding Jim, he knew it was the right call.

The freedom this provided for Jim meant that he could travel and share the message of the gospel with more people, and could devote more time toward fulfilling God's purpose in his life. God also blessed his business, and he was more successful than ever.

Jim has seen miracles, traveled the world, and proclaimed the good news to people everywhere. Though he once walked away from God, God never walked away from Jim. "Through all of the trials I've faced in my life, I have learned to be faithful to the adventure God called me on. I have learned that every battle I've faced has shaped my character in a way that honors God."

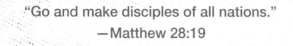

"Go and make disciples of all nations."
—Matthew 28:19

myTask, hisPurpose

You are a man on task whenever you discover and develop your God-given abilities, and sync them with God's purpose to strengthen and serve others.

Aren't you inspired by epic movies of men who live for an extraordinary purpose? When they sacrifice personal safety and comfort for the benefit of others?

Read this charge given by the Baron of Ibelin (a castle near Jerusalem in the days of the Crusaders) from the film *Kingdom of Heaven*, a fictionalized account of the Third Crusade. He gave this charge to his son, Balian, just before he died from a wound he received while saving his son's life:

"Be without fear in the face of your enemy. Be brave and upright because God loves you. Speak the truth always even if it leads to your death. Safeguard the helpless and do no wrong. That is your oath."

Balian went on to become a great leader because of his father's sacrifice.

Such words inspire us. They remind us that men live life best when they live for God and for others. Living this way is not our default setting. Unless we are intentional, we will live for "me, myself, and I," and no one else.

Author C. S. Lewis wrote, "Die before you die. There is no chance after." * Dying to the desire to please oneself first and to the exclusion of everything else is what God means by "die." It's not a physical death, but a choice to live for the well-being of others. Your true life is found in being others-centered instead of being self-centered and self-absorbed. You are most alive inside when you walk with God and when you serve others well. Great men live for a special task that demands much sacrifice. In sacrifice, they find great satisfaction because they have lived for Jesus first, others second, and themselves last.

The remarkable truth is that when you die to selfishness, walk with God, and serve others well, you become fully alive. Satan wants you to be afraid of the word *sacrifice*. He wants to bring images of pain and scarcity to your mind. It will certainly include some pain and trouble. A sacrifice has to include some actual sacrifice. In the sacrifice is where you find true, real, full life! Don't recoil from sacrifice.

God has a divine task for you. It will require you to sacrifice on behalf of others. When you sacrifice for God's purposes, you gain everything!

---

* C.S. Lewis, *Till We Have Faces* (Grand Rapids, Mich.: Eerdmanns, 1976), 279.

CHAPTER 14

My Task

The obvious question is, "What is my task?" If my task is going to make me come alive, let's get to it, right? While the question is obvious, the answer seldom is. There's a reason for that.

You are not a robot. You are a young man with an individual set of fingerprints. You are uncommon, an original. God never makes a copy. Since He took such care to custom-make you, He wants you to relate with Him in a very personal way. God wants your heart. He's going to take you on a customized quest to discover your special task.

To that end, He's going to call you into adventures so you will trust Him and learn that His intentions toward you are always and forever good. He's going to lead you into battles to strengthen your character and fill you with power. As you are ready, He'll reveal your task little by little. Discovering your task is a journey of faith as you build trust in Jesus.

But like any journey, it starts with a first step.

What Makes Me Come Alive?

Discover what makes you come alive. Really alive!

What are the things you most enjoy doing? Is it being in the wild, the great outdoors? Hunting? Playing sports? Physical fitness? Do you like building or repairing things? Creating websites, taking photos, building computers? Playing a musical instrument? Singing? Composing music or lyrics? Writing short stories, essays, or poems? Acting? Giving things away? Serving at a local soup kitchen? Do you like peace and quiet? What kind of books do you read? What kind of people do you like to learn about? What are your favorite subjects at school? What are your favorite kinds of movies or television programs?

The list of possible questions is nearly endless. So the primary question for you is, "What makes me come alive?"

Your interests are not random. God put them there. The wholesome activities you most enjoy are clues to your special task, so enjoy them and explore interests, activities, or hobbies that you think might be fun. If you get into them and decide they aren't for you, fulfill your commitment and move on to something new. After a while you'll start locking in on those activities you most enjoy.

In and of themselves, these interests are not usually sufficient to determine your task. For example, just because you absolutely love everything about white water rafting doesn't necessarily mean your task is to become a full-time guide. When you combine your interests with the adventure God has for you, they reveal a lot. American theologian and civil rights activist, Howard Thurman said it best, "Don't ask what the world needs. Ask what makes you come alive, and go do it. Because what the world needs is people who have come alive."

When you do wholesome things that move or inspire you, listen in those moments for the voice of God because He's there. That emotion signals His presence. He wants to connect with you in that

> "The Lord your God is with you, the Mighty Warrior who saves. He will take great delight in you; in his love he will no longer rebuke you, but will rejoice over you with singing." —Zephaniah 3:17

very instant and let you know you are the apple of His eye. When your favorite team wins the championship game and you jump and shout excitedly, turn that into a prayer of thanks because God is calling out the winner in you. In those moments of pure adrenaline, listen for the voice of God. He's impressed with the music you compose, impressed that you reached that mountain peak and are surveying the beauty below, impressed that you won the cross-country meet. So in those moments when you swell with pride, let God know how much you love Him and then listen. You'll hear Him say, "Well done. Well done, My son!"

While your interests may not be sufficient to define your special task, God will most certainly use them to relate with you personally. He'll use your interests to lead you on adventures and to win battles. He will use your interests to make you come alive to Him. That is exactly what the world needs!

Aren't you glad God has no intention of giving you a boring task? He wants to give you a task that you'll spring from bed each morning to live out, that makes you come alive!

What Am I Good At?

King David of Israel wrote a poem that included this refrain: "I praise you because I am fearfully and wonderfully made; your works are wonderful, I know that full well" (Psalm 139:14).

God has intricately pieced together everything that makes you unique. As you discover the exceptional qualities that God has built into you, you'll gain clues about your task. You have strengths, personality traits, and spiritual gifts that are uniquely you.

Discover your strengths

God has given you a series of personal abilities that are directly related to the task He has for you. As you focus your time and energy on developing your strengths, your life will become more meaningful and fulfilling. Generally speaking, the earlier in life you learn what these strengths are the better.

> The more you can focus your time and energy on developing your strengths instead of your limitations, the greater your personal fulfillment will be.

A good way to discover your areas of strength is to talk with adults who know you well and care about you. Ask them these head, heart, and hands questions:

- Head: In what areas am I mentally sharp? Is it math? Words to write or speak? Problem solving? Planning and organizing? Designing? Creative thinking? Philosophy?

- Heart: When am I at my most passionate and vibrant? Is it when I play music? When I help others? When I'm socializing? When I'm studying or reading?

- Hands: What physical activities do I excel at? Sports? Crafts? Mechanics? Using tools? Music? Art? Building things? Website design? Photography?

You have strengths in each of these areas—head, heart, and hands. Exploring these will help you connect your desires with your strengths.

Discover your personality traits

You are unique! But we know your personality will have themes in common with others. For instance, you might be the in-charge, detailed, outgoing, or laid back guy. Everyone has one of these traits as their primary and another as their secondary.

Paul was the in-charge guy. Moses was detailed. Peter was outgoing. Abraham was laid back. God made every one of them different, but each fulfilled His special task. It's easy to look at others and wish you were more like them and less like you. But it is best to live with a thankful heart that God made you as He did. Determine to be the best version of you possible; don't copy others.

The best way to discover your personality traits is to, once again, discuss them with an adult who knows you well. Look to your parents, but also look to church leaders, pastors, or teachers who have taken time to invest in you. They will all likely have a different perspective, and you can piece their thoughts together with what God has revealed to you about yourself. In doing this, the puzzle of your personality becomes complete.

Note that this process can be intimidating, and sometimes it can overwhelm you. The key is not to focus too much on negative or positive traits. Instead, ask yourself these questions:

- Am I more comfortable being the leader of a group or being a follower of a good leader?

- Am I more of a "big picture" person, or are the little things really important to me?

- Do I enjoy new situations and people, or does it take me a while to find my comfort zone?

- Am I usually intensely focused and driven, or am I a person who takes things as they come?

Your personality is complex, unique, and evolving. While you may have some of the same personality traits all your life, others may grow and change as you grow into the man God envisions you to be. Don't be afraid to explore the unique gifts God has given you.

Discover your spiritual gifts

The Bible tells us the church is like a body. Each part is vital. You are an important member of the church, and to do your part, God gives you spiritual gifts. Spiritual gifts are special, specific tools that are given to believers for the building up of the church body (Ephesians 4:11–13).

The Bible lists many spiritual gifts of various kinds. Some are gifts to fulfill a particular ministry such as preaching, teaching, or evangelizing. Others are given to allow God to speak through His people like prophecy, tongues, and interpretation. There are gifts that demonstrate the great power of the Spirit like miracles, powers, and healing. There are gifts of wisdom, knowledge, discernment, leadership, mercy, and encouragement. First Corinthians 12–14, Ephesians 4, and Romans 12 give detailed teaching on the different gifts of the Spirit, their purposes, and how they should be used.

The most essential element of all the gifts is described in 1 Corinthians 13. In the middle of chapters teaching the proper purposes and uses of spiritual gifts, Paul writes, "Now these three remain: faith, hope, and love. But the greatest of these is love" (1 Corinthians 13:13). If you don't have love for God and for others, it doesn't matter how skilled you are, how gifted you have become, or how hard you have worked. Love, characterized by sacrificially and selflessly sharing your strength with others, is the ultimate gift of the Holy Spirit.

Who Do I Talk To?

Once you have thought about what makes you come alive and have taken time to discover your strengths, personality traits, and spiritual gifts, share what you have learned and what you are feeling with your parents, pastors, and mentors. The adults in your life have wisdom and experience to help you interpret what you have learned and take the proper steps to use your discoveries to the greatest effect.

Also, learn from people of the past who share your passions. You'll find stories in the Bible, other books, magazines, and movies. You'll be introduced to them in history and literature classes, and watching historical features and documentaries is a great way to learn about heroes from the past. Discover their strengths, how they overcame adversity, the source of their courage, and how they responded to failure. Did they finish strong? Why or why not? What can you take away from their experiences? If you learn the good, the bad, and the ugly from others you can lead a better and brighter life. You'll avoid their mistakes and take advantage of their successes. Discuss what you pick up with your parents, pastors, and mentors.

Above all, talk with God. He's ready to listen, and as you let Him, He will lead you on adventures and through battles that will shape your understanding of who you are. Even as God is leading you, rely on a spiritually mature adult to mentor and help you, especially if you get stuck or begin to drift.

What's Next?

As you make these discoveries, look for opportunities to sharpen your strengths, develop your talents, and exercise your gifts. Don't fall into the trap of spending lots of time on your weaknesses. Yes, file off the rough edges of those weaknesses that hurt you or others, but if you spend all your time on these, you will not live in your strengths. Focus on improving your strengths and chasing those things that make you come alive. In other words, better your strengths by using them to serve others. The talents and the passions God has given you are His gifts to you. Your gift back to Him is what you do with them. Determine to become the best version of you possible. That is God's heart!

Now let me give a word of warning. These steps of discovery will be a battle of sorts. Satan will want you to think, "Oh, that's too much work." If he can discourage you, he can keep you aimless. He'll try to confuse or frustrate you along the way. Don't give up! He may try to burden you with worry, "Can I actually get direction from God?" Yes, you can! God has a special task for you, and the journey is important because it will bring you closer to Jesus, which is the last thing the devil wants. If the journey were not important, God would have simply attached a tag on your toe at birth, describing what you were to do. However, that wouldn't deepen your trust and passion for Christ.

Remember, Jesus wants your heart more than anything, so don't minimize the importance of this journey and don't put it off. Your future is expecting you.

In Your Own Words:

1. Describe something positive you've done lately that made you come alive. Why did you feel so passionate about what you did? How did it make you and others feel?

2. As you discover your strengths, personality traits, and spiritual gifts, talk with your parents and mentors about how you can effectively grow stronger and use them to fulfill your potential.

3. Take a few moments right now and ask God to help you to discover His design for your life and find what makes you come alive.

In My Experience:

One of the great opportunities of your preteen and teen years is that you get to dream and explore your interests. Take full advantage of this time.

Growing up in Bolivia, I discovered my love of planning, leading, organizing, and public speaking. I learned it on the go. At first the idea scared me. I'll never forget the feeling of terror that gripped me when I was invited to help a church start a Royal Rangers group to mentor boys. I was just a teen! I translated materials from English to Spanish and prepared the best I could. Several months later, after training the leaders, we launched our first meeting and the rest, as they say, is history. I've been involved in mentoring future men around the world ever since. Courageously confronting my fears made all the difference.

I also enjoyed representing my class on student council for several years in high school. The role of representative fit me well. I wasn't sufficiently popular to win election as class president, for example. But since representing my class required actual work, which I love, no one ever challenged me for the job. I discovered how much I enjoyed raising funds, planning events, and relating with my peers and the staff and faculty on special initiatives. This love for servant leadership led me recently to complete a master's degree in organizational leadership.

Other things that made me come alive as a teen were hiking and camping, playing guitar, and jogging. These are activities I enjoy to this day. But there were other things I tried and later dropped. I became quite skilled at playing piano, but didn't enjoy it.

Find ways to discover your interests. You are in a season of life where you don't have to be fully committed to anything yet. So if you try something for a semester and realize it's not for you, drop it and move on. But when you discover things that make you come alive, set and reach some goals that will challenge you to have fun and learn new things. Above all, don't do nothing. Keep trying to discover activities and interests that will capture your imagination.

Learning what makes you come alive is like learning to ride a bike. You start with lots of help and encouragement, especially when you scrape a knee or elbow. Relying on training wheels helps, and before you know it you've mastered something you love and that will take you places.

So go ahead, explore and take some risks. Believe in yourself the way God does. Ask Him to guide you toward those things that make you come alive.

For further information on discovering your personality, strengths, and spiritual gifts, check out the following websites:

- www.ClasServices.com
  Author Florence Littauer has written a fun book on the personalities called *Personality Plus* which includes a simple personality test. You can obtain a copy of the test from her webstore.

- www.Strengths-Explorer.com
  Ideal for boys ages 10–14

- www.StrengthsQuest.com
  Ideal for guys ages 15–17

- www.StrengthsFinder.com
  Ideal for adults

- www.churchgrowth.org/analysis/intro.php
  This website offers a free and quick online assessment that will help you discover your spiritual gifts.

CHAPTER 15

God's Purpose

Paul, that take-charge guy who wrote a bunch of the New Testament, said this about Jesus, "It is for freedom that Christ has set us free" (Galatians 5:1). Specifically, you are God's mission and purpose. He came to set you free so you could really live!

Before Jesus died on the cross for our sins and rose from the dead, humankind was under the domain of Satan. Now, Christ has rescued us. When you give Him your life and choose to follow Him instead of going your own way, He begins to set matters straight in your life. That is God's purpose—to put back together what Satan broke in your life.

On a trip to Jericho, Jesus told everyone why He came to earth, "The Son of Man came to seek and to save the lost" (Luke 19:10). Jesus came to set our lives straight. As He traveled during His earthly ministry, Jesus was always looking to love and forgive people, to deliver them from demonic oppression, to heal them, to make them laugh, to give them hope, and to bring justice and equality to the forgotten and oppressed.

While attending the synagogue in Nazareth, His hometown, Jesus read from an Old Testament scroll that foretold His mission this way: God's Son was to heal the brokenhearted and to set the captives free (Isaiah 61:1). John 3:17 says that God sent Jesus into the world not to condemn it, but to save it. That is the opposite of everything Satan brings to the world. Satan enslaves, but Jesus saves! John 10:10 says, "The thief comes only to steal and kill and destroy; I have come that they may have life, and have it to the full."

From these verses we gather a clear picture of God's purpose for sending His Son. Jesus came:

- To seek and save what was lost

- To heal the brokenhearted

- To set captives free

- To save the world

- To give full life

To sum it up, Jesus came to set things right. He started this mission, but now He intends for you to continue it. You are His ally to let people see Christ's love radiate from your life, to help them discover a personal relationship with God through faith in Jesus Christ, to help those who feel hopeless and forgotten by loving and helping them get back on their feet, and to help them find the full and exhilarating life Jesus promises.

The Great Commission is "Go into all the world and preach the gospel to all creation" (Mark 16:15). Your commission may very well include preaching or teaching, but there are many ways to share the gospel with others. You must use both words and actions to declare the message of Jesus.

Hal Donaldson started Convoy of Hope to reduce human suffering across America and around the world, and to help people find Jesus. His organization is able to respond quickly when natural disasters upset people's lives and to bring them hope. By providing food, medical care, and disaster relief, they are able to reach people for Jesus who would otherwise be lost. Convoy of Hope puts faith into action.

Donaldson is continuing Jesus' mission and so must you. You won't be able to set everything straight by yourself, but one day God will finish the mission that Jesus started and we continued. Sin and sickness and hurts will be no more!

> "He who was seated on the throne said, 'I am making everything new!'"
> —Revelation 21:5

In the meantime, you are commissioned to continue Jesus' work. You are expected to be His agent and serve others with all the strength that God gives you through the power of His Holy Spirit.

In Your Own Words:

1. Look up and read the following verses: Isaiah 61:1–3; Luke 19:10; Galatians 5:1; John 3:17; 10:10; Revelation 21:5. Create a one-sentence description of Jesus' life purpose.

2. How can your strengths and abilities further Jesus' purposes in this world?

In My Experience:

Would you rather be treated by a doctor who has never been sick or by one who has experienced sickness or an accident at least once? If you're like me, you prefer the latter because that doctor is probably going to be more gentle and caring.

The Bible tells us Jesus is able to sympathize with our weaknesses because He suffered and was tempted in every way just like we are, and yet He never sinned (Hebrews 2:18; 4:15). Jesus is moved by our human condition because He experienced it himself. In our own lives it often takes personal hardship to better understand what others are going through.

Growing up, I experienced several traumatic accidents. Once, when I was about eleven years old, I fell into a very large cactus while hiking in Bolivia. There were no trails in the area I was exploring, and the steep, one hundred foot climb from the valley floor was treacherous. As I neared the top, the dry clay-like dirt failed to provide the grip my feet needed and I began to slide and lose my balance. I feared falling backward and rolling to the bottom. So I quickly turned, fell on my rear to slow myself, and hoped to find some brush to grab.

What I saw immediately before me was not good. I was falling into a large cactus at least twice my size and there was no way to stop it. I put my right hand out to shield my face. In an instant I hit the plant and it completely broke my fall. My right hand and arm were covered with hundreds of thorns. My head, shoulders, chest, and legs were all reeling in pain. I cried for help, but there was no one. The plant I had fallen into was much larger than me and I still had to get out of it.

The pain was overwhelming and more than once I nearly passed out. Finally I freed myself and laid in the dirt moaning and crying. I slowly began to pull thorns from my body. Discouragement was overtaking me. I still had to safely make my way back into the valley I had climbed from and walk nearly two miles home.

Fortunately, the boots I wore protected my feet. When I got home my mom carefully helped me out of my clothes, put me in a hot salt bath, and gently removed the remaining thorns.

It appeared we had gotten them all. But little did we know two thorns in my right wrist had broken off well under the surface of the skin. At first I assumed my wrist was sore from the fall itself. But the pain grew and an infection set in. An X-ray revealed there was a small thorn about an eighth of an inch long and another about three-fourths of an inch long lodged in the joint of my wrist. My parents arranged for immediate surgery, and the thorns were removed. But it took weeks for the infection and the incision to heal.

From this experience I learned empathy, that is, caring about and feeling the pain of others. Before that I wouldn't have even pretended to be concerned for you if you were sick, much less feel authentic compassion. The battles you and I face help us relate better with hurting people.

Jesus put himself in our world so He could experience all of our human emotions and weaknesses. But it wasn't enough for Him to feel it. He had the power to reverse the pain, and He set things in motion to restore us to our original relationship with Him. What Jesus started will be fully accomplished when we are in heaven.

In the meantime He wants you to discover the things that make you come alive and use them to further His purposes. His mission is to set things right. What makes you come alive can deliver Jesus' life to those He cares about.

Jesus' mission is to fix what the devil has broken in people's lives. I think of human trafficking, of young girls who are forced into prostitution. They are being exploited! Jesus wants to free them. He specializes in seeking out those who have been robbed of their innocence and healing their physical, emotional, and spiritual pain. He accomplishes His task through men like you and me who will share their strength with those who are weak and disadvantaged.

It starts by knowing and caring about Jesus' mission—the mission to seek and to save what has been lost and stolen in people's lives. Then you offer Him what makes you come alive so He can use it to heal those around you. His purpose is your task—to let the whole world know Jesus can set things right in their life if they will invite Him to do so.

CHAPTER 16

The Great Commission

L et's piece it all together. God has given you strengths, personality traits, and spiritual gifts that will uniquely qualify you to accomplish your life's task. It will be something that makes you come alive and that will leverage your best qualities. However, this task does have a specific focus—to continue Jesus' mission.

You are not on this planet just to mind your manners, though hopefully, you will. You are not here just to find a great career and make a good living, though that is very likely. You are certainly not here just to find ways to entertain yourself. You are here to be the man God designed you to be and to share the strength that He gives you with others. Your life's task will influence many people to become followers of Christ. This is your great purpose, your Great Commission.

Charles T. Studd, an 1880s British missionary to China and Africa, said, "Some wish to live within the sound of church or chapel

---

"Go into all the world and preach the good news
to all creation." —Mark 16:15

---

bell; I want to run a rescue shop within a yard of hell." Before becoming a missionary, Studd was a sports celebrity at Cambridge University. Though he loved playing cricket, he knew his greatest purpose was to continue Jesus' mission—to encourage people to love Jesus so they could become all He designed them to be, avoid hell, and spend eternity in heaven with Christ.

So it was with former politician, John Ashcroft. While residing in the Missouri governor's mansion, representing Missouri in the U.S. Senate, and serving as U.S. Attorney General, he was always faithful to continue Jesus' mission. His integrity spoke volumes as he shared his God-given strength with the nation following the terrorist attacks of September 2001.

As it was with Studd and Ashcroft, so it must be with you. Regardless of the life task God leads you into—ministry, politics, business, or something just as outstanding—you are to "run a rescue shop" wherever you live or work.

This will take courage. Serving as a missionary is dangerous. Standing strong for Christ as a public servant can be politically risky. A businessman who designates a large percentage of his income to help the less fortunate will have to be content with fewer possessions.

The alternative is far more dangerous. Finding your sweet spot in life and failing to focus it on continuing Jesus' mission will steer you right back into self-centeredness and dead-end living. However, when you combine all your strengths to "run a rescue shop within a yard of hell" so people can experience freedom in Christ, you become dangerous for a good purpose. There is no better way to live!

In Your Own Words:

1. Read Mark 16:15. Why is it called the Great Commission? Does it apply to you? If so, how?

2. This chapter featured excerpts from the stories of Charles T. Studd and John Ashcroft who excelled in their strengths and passions while accomplishing God's purposes. Can you think of at least two other people you know personally or have learned about who have done the same? How have their stories influenced you?

3. What can you do today to fulfill the Great Commission? What's keeping you from doing it?

In My Experience:

A few years ago, my Uncle Bob passed away and I started to reflect on the fullness of his life. He joined the Marine Corps out of high school the way his older brothers had before him. Once he got out he realized that he really enjoyed working with his hands and so he became a plumber, and a very good one at that. Early in his career, residential air conditioning began to develop. As homes started to move away from the old window units in select rooms of the home to central air and heat that provided climatic control for the entire home, he was on the leading edge of installation and maintenance.

But there was a problem. God was tapping on his shoulder to be involved in ministry to achieve God's purposes. But he fought it. At first I'm not sure he knew how to reconcile his love for working with his hands and this growing call to ministry. Perhaps he was paralyzed by a common misconception that you are only in ministry if you are a full-time pastor, evangelist, missionary, Bible professor, or other professional minister. The truth is you are called into ministry regardless of your career choice. Some of the biblical greats, like Stephen, were not apostles. But they knew God's purposes and prepared themselves equally well for their career and their ministry. These men of God understood that their work allowed them the opportunity to accomplish God's work.

In time, my Uncle Bob decided to pastor a church in rural Missouri. He had finally found the perfect combination, plumber and pastor. The fact is he influenced people for Christ that no one else could have. His impact on the lives of his neighbors was immeasurable. Can you imagine attending your plumber's funeral? His memorial service was packed with people whose lives he had changed for eternity. Real living is doing what makes you come alive within the purposes of Christ.

God's Great Commission requires that you use your life's work, whatever that may be, to influence those around you for Christ. God will direct you to do that in a very unique way. For some that will be full-time ministry as a pastor. A musician will glorify God in his lyrics. A police officer will serve and protect the public with integrity and justice. And a plumber will impact countless lives with the good news. Regardless of the means, the mission is to be God's ally in your area of influence.

"GO AND MAKE DISCIPLES OF ALL NATIONS."

Matthew 28:19

Take Your Task Everywhere

One of Christ's final instructions to His followers was, "Go and make disciples of all nations" (Matthew 28:19). That means you have the opportunity to help people put their trust in Jesus Christ and become fully devoted followers of Him. Once they come to faith, they will have questions and need guidance. The following six illustrated lessons will equip you to help them.

Lesson #1—Follow Christ

Purpose: Through His life, death, and resurrection, you are able to have a relationship with Jesus Christ.

At one time, God and man had such a close relationship that they could talk to each other face-to-face. Unfortunately, man chose to sin. That sin created a great separation between God and man, and as much as man wanted to have a relationship with God again, there was nothing he could

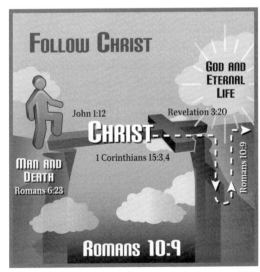

do to fix the relationship. Man's sin had created an impassable gulf between man and God. The ultimate result of that break in the relationship meant that you and I now have to face death. The punishment for my sin and your sin is death, being eternally separated from relationship with God (Romans 6:23).

God loved us so much that He sent His only Son, Jesus, to die on the cross in our place in order to bridge the gap that separates us from God (Romans 5:8). Jesus, in obedience to His Father, came to earth as a man, lived a life without sin, died on the cross to pay sin's debt, and then rose again in victory over death (1 Corinthians 15:3–4). In doing so, He created a bridge across the great divide that separates you and me from God. That bridge is faith in Jesus as Friend and Leader of your life (John 1:12).

What's even more awesome is that Jesus wants everyone to accept Him and cross the bridge into a new relationship with God. He is asking all people to open up their hearts and receive Him as Savior. He is knocking at your heart's door right now asking if He can have a relationship with you (Revelation 3:20). All you have to do is open the door. The way you open the door is through believing in your heart that Jesus is Lord and saying it out loud with faith in your heart (Romans 10:9). God wants a relationship with you, and Jesus is the only way to have that relationship.

Lesson #2—You Can Know

Purpose: Once you believe in Christ, you are adopted into the family of God and your name is written in the Lamb's Book of Life.

Once you believe in Jesus, you become part of the family of God (Romans 8:15). You don't stop being a part of your current family. Your parents are still your parents and your siblings are still your siblings, but you also join God's family. When you join God's family, you get all the rights and privileges of everyone else in the family. That starts with not having to worry about death anymore.

When you believe in Jesus and become part of His family, God gives you eternal life (John 5:24). Now, that doesn't mean your body will not die someday. Everyone dies. When you die physically, your soul will go immediately to be with God. The eternal life that God gives us allows us to spend all of eternity in heaven with God and with everyone else in God's family.

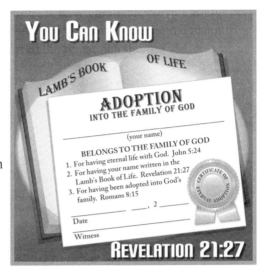

In order to enter heaven, your name must be written in the Lamb's Book of Life (Revelation 21:27). The Lamb's Book of Life is where the name of everyone who is in God's family is written down. When you die, if your name is in that book, you can go to heaven. You definitely want your name in the book. If you have accepted Jesus into your life, then you are set! The minute you believe in Jesus and confess Him as Lord, your name is written in that book.

Lesson #3—Live Free

Purpose: As a member of God's family, you have the opportunity to live free from sin because of Jesus' sacrifice for you on the cross.

Since you have believed and been adopted into the family of God, you should live like you are part of His family. God gives us a gift, the Holy Spirit, to give us strength and help us obey God's commands. The Bible literally calls the Holy Spirit our "Helper" because He is with us to help us. The Holy Spirit will help us stay free from sin.

Living free from sin starts by forgiving others for the wrong things they have done to us (Matthew 6:14). Jesus said that if we forgive

165

others, God forgives us. Forgiving others can be very difficult, especially if they have treated you very badly. Holding on to grudges is not what God wants for us. In order to love others, we must forgive them when they hurt us.

As you continue to follow Christ, you must daily separate yourself from sin (Proverbs 28:13). Temptation is common to everyone. However, you should avoid situations that open you up to be tempted. Part of staying free from sin is not voluntarily walking into the situations where it is easy to sin. It also means that you should surround yourself with people who want to do the right things. When you do sin, you need to confess your sins to God immediately, and He will forgive you (1 John 1:9). This is all part of staying free from sin. If you never confess your sins, you can never be free from them.

As a member of God's family (1 John 2:1), you will absolutely be forgiven because of Jesus' sacrifice on the cross. The moment you confess your sins to God, the blood of Jesus washes your sins away (I John 1:7). It does not cover over your sins like paint over a stain but washes your sins away completely so they don't exist anymore.

Lesson #4—Run the Race

Purpose: Being a follower of Christ requires recognizing that He is in control of your life and you are committed to following His plans.

Now that you are a believer in Christ, free from sin and living a life with the desire to follow Him, you have the responsibility to complete the work that Christ left for you to do. When Jesus lived here on the earth, He came to finish the work of God in the world (John 4:34). That

work was to make a way for man to once again have a relationship with God. Jesus' life, death, and resurrection completed the work of God. Now you have a job to do, and that job is to tell others that there is a way to receive forgiveness and have a relationship with God through Jesus Christ.

In order to do that, you must first agree to cooperate and work His plan (2 Timothy 4:7). Some people want to live their lives the way they choose. God has a plan for you that is better than anything you could ever come up with on your own, and it includes finishing His work.

Second, you need to rededicate yourself to God and His work daily (Luke 9:23). You must have a daily relationship with Him. This daily relationship you have with Him will allow you to know Jesus and His plans (Philippians 3:8). If you are close to Christ and spend your days developing your relationship with Him, the Holy Spirit will help you know His plans for your life. Finally, you must remember to always acknowledge Jesus as Lord (John 20:28). He is the one in control of your life, and He deserves to receive honor from you. By living your life this way, you are prepared to share the good news of the gospel and complete His work.

Lesson #5—Conversations That Bring Life

Purpose: Through the study of God's Word, you can grow closer to God through obeying His commands and following Christ's example.

God has given you a wonderful gift to help you grow spiritually. The gift is the Bible. Reading your Bible every day will help you grow closer to Jesus as you learn more about Him and the plan that He has for your life. The Bible is God's great love letter to you. It explains how much He loves you, and what

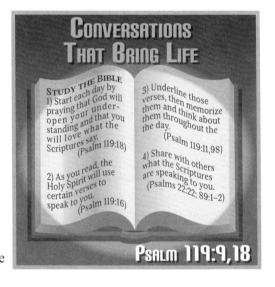

CONVERSATIONS THAT BRING LIFE

STUDY THE BIBLE
1) Start each day by praying that God will open your understanding and that you will love what the Scriptures say.
(Psalm 119:18)

2) As you read, the Holy Spirit will use certain verses to speak to you.
(Psalm 119:16)

3) Underline those verses, then memorize them and think about them throughout the day.
(Psalm 119:11,98)

4) Share with others what the Scriptures are speaking to you.
(Psalms 22:22; 89:1-2)

PSALM 119:9, 18

Jesus did to make sure you could accept His love by developing a relationship with Him. The Scriptures are alive and powerful and will speak to your heart about things in your life.

Here are some tips to help you study and understand the Bible. Start each day by praying that God would open your eyes and ears to understand and love what the Scriptures say (Psalm 119:18). As you read, the Holy Spirit will use certain verses to speak to you (Psalm 119:16). Whenever this happens, underline them in your Bible so you can come back to them again later. Then, memorize them and think about them throughout the day (Psalm 119:11,98).

Having God's Word constantly on your heart and in your mind will help you avoid sin. Remember these Scriptures throughout your day, and allow them to guide you in how you worship God, what you ask from Him, and how to show your thankfulness. The Scriptures will give you guidance on what is truly important in your life. Finally, tell others what the Scriptures are speaking to you (Psalm 22:22; 89:1–2). Sharing what God is doing in your life will encourage others by allowing them to see the Holy Spirit at work in your life.

Lesson #6—Talk to God

Purpose: Through prayer, you can worship and interact with God, seeing your needs met and hearing His voice.

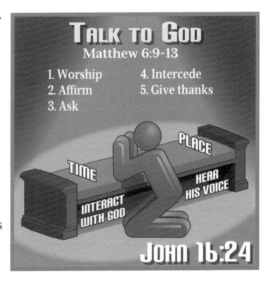

In order to grow closer to Jesus each day, in addition to reading the Bible, you must pray and have daily conversations with God. Imagine having a friend that you never talked to. They wouldn't be much of a friend, would they? You build relationships through hanging out with people and having conversations with them. It is no different with God. You can talk to Him every day, at any time of day, and if you listen you can hear Him talking to you. He wants you to talk to Him, and to depend on Him for answers to your needs (John 16:24).

When Jesus was on earth, He provided an example of how to pray. It is referred to as the Lord's Prayer and is found in Matthew 6:9–13. It is a great example of how to pray. It starts with worshipping God, telling Him how great He is (verse 9). We should always approach God with an attitude of worship. It is true that He is our Friend, but He is also our Leader and worthy of respect and honor.

Then, we should affirm that we believe in His plan and are committed to it (verse 10). Being committed to the purposes of God is part of being in relationship with Him. It is then that we begin to ask God for our needs (verse 11). It is important to understand why we ask after we affirm—God will give us whatever we ask for as long as it is according to His plan. By affirming God's purposes and our place in them, we know that we ask for the right things and God will give them to us.

Next, Christ teaches us to intercede for the important things in our lives (verse 12). We must confess our sins and ask God to forgive us, as well as ask Him to deliver us from the attacks of the enemy and the traps that Satan sets for us. Think about all the blessings and great things you have going on in your life. Those things only exist because God gave them to you. It's important that our prayers demonstrate a thankful heart.

From a Deadly Car Crash Rises a Convoy of Hope: Hal Donaldson

The lasting legacy of Hal Donaldson cannot be measured. He has, quite simply, changed the world through his spirit of generosity, his dedication to Christ, and his determination to make a difference. He has also permanently imprinted his world-changing view on my heart. His story covers devastating lows and unimaginable heights, and clearly shows what God's Spirit can do when we choose to go on an adventure with Him.

Hal was only twelve when his father was tragically killed in an auto accident. Hal, along with his brothers Steve and David, will never forget the day. From that day forward his mother was left with the challenge of raising three young boys alone. Finding work was difficult, and financial hardships set in immediately. The family soon went on welfare just to make ends meet.

Hal remembers, "When you're twelve years old and you lose a parent, you really begin to ask God the hard questions: 'Why did this happen? Why me?' For a long time, my mother was grieving, and we didn't want to burden her with our questions. So we often turned to our mentors, Royal Rangers leaders, for help and answers, and they were there for us."

Hal credits his mentors for helping him maintain his faith in God through his father's death and the subsequent struggles the family endured. "I was the oldest boy in our family, and in a situation like ours, you have to grow up pretty quickly. I began looking for people to emulate, for role models, and I found a lot of men to copy in my church. When you've lost your dad, the cupboards are empty, you can't afford a haircut, and your clothes are not up to par, it's very easy to feel inferior. But my mentors really took me and my two brothers under their wings and nurtured us. They gave me confidence," remembers Hal.

"It would have been easy to become bitter over what had happened, but fortunately we had a church family and strong men that took

Convoy of Hope, founded by Hal Donaldson (left), provides food and humanitarian assistance to impoverished and needy people all around the world.

care of us and really showed us the love of Christ in practical ways. Through it all, I learned God had a purpose in everything He did, and I resolved to keep my faith in Him no matter what."

In 1994, God placed it in Hal's heart to begin a ministry of providing groceries to families in need. One day, with a pickup truck and a load of groceries, Hal went into the most needy areas of his community and began passing out food. Over time, others joined in the effort, and nearly twenty years later, Convoy of Hope serves millions each year.

Today, Convoy of Hope provides food and humanitarian assistance to impoverished and needy people all around the world. Over the last ten years, this international effort, one of the largest relief organizations in the world, has mobilized over 200,000 volunteers to serve thirty million people, sharing the love of Christ with them in tangible ways.

"What started out with just one pickup has now grown into a fleet of semitrucks, a 300,000 square foot warehouse in Springfield, Missouri, and additional warehouses on five continents. We send supplies to our missionaries and national churches all over the world. God continues to bless and multiply this outreach to the poor and suffering," Hal says.

Hal Donaldson is an example of a man who drew strength from pain. It made him better. He learned to relieve his suffering by serving others. In doing so he was extending God's love. It became his career, a calling in fact. It is purpose anchored in God's mission. Hal's abilities are in full use, and he's most alive when he's expressing God's love to the world.

Final Challenge

"The LORD bless you and keep you; the LORD make his face shine on you and be gracious to you; the LORD turn his face toward you and give you peace." —Numbers 6:24–26

CHAPTER 17

Take the Journey!

Becoming a man of God is about becoming the best version of you possible. You were born a male, so God wants you to become an extraordinary man!

Reflect on the journey God is inviting you to take:

- He will take you on ADVENTURE so you learn to love Him and others. He wants you to be great at living the Great Commandment.

- He will forge your CHARACTER as you depend on His power for life and service. He wants you to experience the Great Empowerment of His Holy Spirit.

- He will reveal a special TASK so your life gains influence and focus. He wants you to discover and accept your lead role in His Great Commission.

Are you willing to take the journey? In Mark 4, Jesus tells a parable worth reading carefully as you stand on the cusp of this important journey.

"A farmer went out to sow seed. That is, to generously plant the life-giving Word of God in the hearts of young men.

"As He was scattering the seed, some fell along the path, and the birds came and ate it up. This is like the young man who hears the Word but allows Satan to steal it away without a fight.

"Some seed fell on rocky places where it did not have much soil. It sprang up quickly because the soil was shallow, but when the sun came up, the plants were scorched and withered because their root system was shallow and had no water. This is like the young man who receives the Word with enthusiasm. However, he never spends the time to establish spiritual disciplines, he is never willing to do difficult things, and the Word never set roots into his heart. This caused the new sprouts to wither. When trouble or persecution comes because of the Word, he quickly falls away and goes back to old living.

"Other seed fell among thorns, which grew up and choked the plants so that they did not bear grain. This is the young man who hears the Word but takes his eyes off the prize of becoming like Jesus. He allows the worries of this life, the deceitfulness of image and peer pressure, and the desires for less important things to come in and choke out the Word, making his life unfruitful.

"Still other seed fell on good soil. It came up, grew, and produced a crop, multiplying thirty, sixty, or even a hundred times. This is the young man who hears the Word, accepts it, and becomes the man God intended him to be. This young man is amazed, and he is amazing! He devoted his heart to Jesus with high expectations and discovers that God regularly far exceeds his wildest dreams. His life is full and overflowing!"

Paraphrase based on Mark 4:3–8; 15–20

There are some valuable lessons to be learned from this passage.

Be Good Soil

The parable tells you four kinds of young men received God's Word:

- One accepted it but didn't put up a fight when Satan came to steal the seed away. Being passive cost him his life.

- Then, there was the guy who accepted it, saw some early results, but wasn't willing to do the challenging things that make men strong. He wanted it to come easy, but since that is not how life works, he withered up and died.

- Next, there was the man who took his eyes off the prize of becoming like Jesus, the ultimate man, and after a while, he gave up. His concern for image and what people might think of him cost him dearly.

- The last guy fought off the devil, did the hard things to gain strength to share with the world, gave sacrificially, and became the young man God intended. He found real life!

What's it going to be? To be the last guy, the successful one, you'll have to follow God on ADVENTURES, forge your CHARACTER through hardship, and journey with God to discover your life TASK. By doing this—by going on adventures, fighting the battles, and discovering your purpose—you'll be doing the things that make you good soil, a heart ready to receive everything God has for you.

Trust the Father

Your Heavenly Father scatters seed generously. You can take on adventures, battles, and special tasks with total confidence. They will be filled with dangers and risks and will demand great sacrifice and uncommon love, but Jesus won't hold out on you. Your obedient faith will produce results in your life that will far exceed your investment because God is bountiful and generous!

Take No Shortcuts

In the parable, the guys who took shortcuts lost. Being passive has no place in your masculine journey. It's not even in your vocabulary. Hesitate to do tough things? Not at all! You laugh at challenges, stare them down, and overcome. Fear others and what they'll say because you are determined to be a godly man? Not a chance. You laid that one to rest a long time ago. You are far more interested in what God thinks of you than in the opinions of others. An adventure with God will take you on a road that's far less traveled. There are no shortcuts to character. The hard journey to discover your task is far better than a life of aimless wandering. Your pledge is, "With God's help I will do my best." Shortcuts lead to second best. Only God's best is your destiny.

Now that you know how God builds a man, are you willing to go on adventure with Him? Are you willing to let the Holy Spirit shape your character? Are you willing to discover and assume your life task? You can ACT like a man! Let God build your life. If you do, it will be full of exciting ADVENTURE, strong CHARACTER, and a special TASK. That is what being a godly man is all about—becoming the best version of you, the best man you can be. You were born a male, so let God shape you into the extraordinary man He wants you to become!

Are you ready? Go!

Subject Index